A life well-designed is a life well-lived.

GW01018163

Vincent Fournier
from the series „Flora Incognita"
UltraHD photo print under acrylic glass | Solid Wood ArtBox, maple white
16 x 22 inches | printed by WhiteWall.com

Photography in perfection

For everyone who loves photography. For more than 15 years, artists and discerning photographers worldwide have placed their trust in WhiteWall's photo lab. Winner of TIPA's "Best Photo Lab Worldwide", we offer unmatched quality through the combination of traditional development and the latest technologies. Discover our printing passion at WhiteWall.com

 **WHITE WALL**

The Design Issue
Summer 2024

Columns

16

Features

56

The Design Issue
Summer 2024

Features

122

132

The PhotoBook Review

151

Aperture's Design issue
features three covers:

David Hartt, *Olimpia*, 2022
(See page 46)

Luigi Ghirri, from the series
Ferrari, 1985–90
(See page 56)

Dayanita Singh, from
the series *Studio Mumbai*,
2019–ongoing
(See page 68)

Subscribe to *Aperture* and
read more at aperture.org.

Richard Misrach

June 22 - August 3, 2024

MARC SELWYN FINE ART

9953 South Santa Monica Boulevard, Beverly Hills, CA 90212

Aperture is a nonprofit publisher dedicated to creating insight, community, and understanding through photography. Established in 1952 to advance "creative thinking, significantly expressed in words and photographs," Aperture champions photography's vital role in nurturing curiosity and encouraging a more just, tolerant society.

Aperture (ISSN 0003-6420) is published quarterly, in spring, summer, fall, and winter, at 548 West 28th Street, 4th Floor, New York, NY 10001. Subscriptions are $75/year. For delivery in Canada, add $20; for other countries, add $35. Single copies may be purchased for $24.95. To subscribe or buy single copies, visit aperture.org. Periodicals postage paid at New York and additional mailing offices. POSTMASTER: Send address changes to Aperture, PO Box 3000, Denville, NJ 07834. For customer service, please call 866-457-4603 (US and Canada) or email custsvc_aperture@fulcoinc.com. Newsstand distribution in the US is handled by CMG. For international distribution, contact Central Books, centralbooks.com. Other inquiries, email orders@aperture.org or call 212-505-5555.

Credits for "Timeline," pp. 14–15: Draper: Courtesy the Draper Family Collection, New York University; Whipple: Courtesy the Library of Congress; De La Rue: © Victoria and Albert Museum; Smillie: Courtesy the Smithsonian Institution; Nasmyth and Carpenter: Courtesy the University of St Andrews Libraries and Museums; TV moon: Courtesy the Museum of Fine Arts, Houston. Credits for "Curriculum," pp. 24–25: *Mapas Abiertos* and "Discarded Photographs": Courtesy Alejandro Cartagena; Harvey: Courtesy Roger Cremers/laif/Redux

Library of Congress Catalog Card No: 58-30845.

Support has been provided by members of Aperture's Magazine Council: Jon Stryker and Slobodan Randjelović, Susan and Thomas Dunn, Kate Cordsen and Denis O'Leary, and Michael W. Sonnenfeldt, MUUS Collection.

ISBN 978-1-59711-567-4

Printed in Turkey by Ofset Yapimevi

aperture

The Magazine of Photography and Ideas

Editor in Chief
Michael Famighetti
Senior Editor
Brendan Embser
Associate Managing Editor
Varun Nayar
Copy Editors
Hilary Becker, Donna Ghelerter, Chris Peterson
Production Director
Minjee Cho
Production Manager
Andrea Chlad
Press Supervisor
Ali Taptık
Contributing Editor, The PhotoBook Review
Noa Lin

Art Direction, Design & Typefaces
A2/SW/HK, London

Publisher
Dana Triwush
magazine@aperture.org

Director of Corporate Partnerships
Flynn Murray
fmurray@aperture.org

Brand Partnerships Consultant
Isabelle Friedrich McTwigan
imctwigan@aperture.org

Advertising
Elizabeth Morina
emorina@aperture.org

Executive Director, Aperture
Sarah Hermanson Meister

Minor White, Editor and Publisher (1952–1974)
Michael E. Hoffman, Publisher and Executive Director (1964–2001)
Melissa Harris, Editor in Chief (2002–2012)
Chris Boot, Executive Director (2011–2021)
Lesley A. Martin, Founder and Publisher, The PhotoBook Review (2011–2021)

aperture.org

"To Prove that I Exist"

Melissa Shook's Daily Self-Portraits 1972–1973

March 9–August 4, 2024

March 19, 1973

March 20, 1973

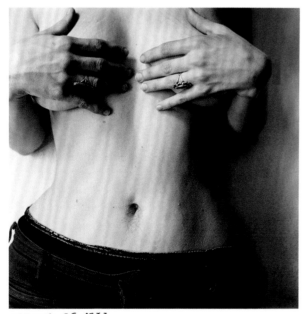

March 29, 1973

March 29, 1973

Melissa Shook, American (1939-2020). *March 19, 1973, March 20, 1973, March 29, 1973, and March 29, 1973*. Gelatin Silver prints, approximately 4 1/2 × 4 3/8 inches. The Nelson-Atkins Museum of Art, Gift of the Hall Family Foundation, 2015.20.147, 2015.20.148, 2015.20.162, and 2015.20.163. © Kristina Shook & The Estate of M. Melissa Shook.

Organized by The Nelson-Atkins Museum of Art, this exhibition is supported by the Hall Family Foundation.

Contributors

VINCE ALETTI ("The Theater of Paul Kooiker," page 132), the former art editor and photography critic at the *Village Voice*, wrote weekly photo exhibition reviews for the *New Yorker* from 2005 to 2016 and now contributes to the magazine's online Photo Booth feature. In 2019, he published *Issues: A History of Photography in Fashion Magazines*. His book *The Drawer* (2022) was named the Aperture/Paris Photo Photobook of the Year in 2023.

THESSALY LA FORCE ("Coreen Simpson: Past Lives," page 110) is a writer based in New York. She is a graduate of the Iowa Writers' Workshop and is a regular contributor to the *New York Times*, *Vogue*, *Harper's Bazaar*, among other publications. She recently published a short story in the book *Five Stories for Philip Guston* (2023).

OLIVIA LAING ("Endnote," page 160) is the celebrated author of several books, including *The Lonely City* (2016), *Crudo* (2018), *Funny Weather: Art in an Emergency* (2020), and *Everybody: A Book About Freedom* (2021). She is a regular contributor to *Aperture*, the *Guardian*, and the *New York Times*, and recently published her latest book, *The Garden Against Time: In Search of a Common Paradise* (2024).

BILLIE MURABEN ("Alice Rawsthorn: Design Touches Everything," page 88) is a design writer and curator based in London. In 2021, she was the assistant curator of the 5th Istanbul Design Biennial. She recently founded Parterre Parterre, a project through which she publishes editions and curates exhibitions with a focus on experimental design and applied arts.

JULIAN ROSE ("Daniel Shea: Empire Plaza," page 78) is a critic of art and architecture and was formerly senior editor at *Artforum*. He has contributed to the *Architectural Review*, *Bookforum*, and *October*, among other publications. As a cofounder of the design studio Formlessfinder, he has exhibited work at the Museum of Modern Art, New York, the Chicago Architecture Biennial, and the Venice Architecture Biennale. His next book, *Building Culture*, an exploration of the architecture of art museums, will be published this fall.

DANIEL SHEA ("Empire Plaza," page 78) is an artist based in New York. His photographs have appeared in the *New Yorker*, *Double*, *Frieze*, and *Fantastic Man*, and his monograph *43–35 10th Street* was published by Kodoji Press in 2018. He has exhibited internationally, including at the US Pavilion of the 2021 Venice Architecture Biennale and Foam Fotografiemuseum, Amsterdam.

DAYANITA SINGH ("Better Living," page 68) is an artist living and working in Delhi. Over her four-decade career, she has made numerous inventive photobooks, including *Sent a Letter* (2008), *Museum Bhavan* (2017), and *Zakir Hussain Maquette* (2019). In 2013, she was one of four artists featured in the German Pavilion at the Venice Biennale, and her photographic project *Museum of Chance* was presented in the exhibition *Surrounds: 11 Installations* at the Museum of Modern Art, New York, in 2019. Singh's retrospective, *Dancing with My Camera*, recently traveled to Germany, Luxembourg, and Portugal.

DAN THAWLEY ("Duro Olowu: Cutting a Figure," page 34) is an editor, curator, and creative director based in Paris. He was the editor in chief of *A Magazine Curated By* from 2010 to 2023, for which he produced collaborations with numerous designers, including Thom Browne, Alessandro Michele, Simone Rocha, and Grace Wales Bonner. The author of *Radical Renaissance 60* (2016), about the fashion executive Renzo Rosso, Thawley is the artistic director of Matter and Shape, a Paris design salon.

ELIZABETH "DORI" TUNSTALL ("Polymode: Poetic Research," page 146) is a design anthropologist, author of *Decolonizing Design: A Cultural Justice Guidebook* (2023), and a leader and consultant through her firm, Dori Tunstall, Inc., which helps organizations diversify their institutional processes.

MIMI ZEIGER ("David Hartt: Paradise Lost," page 46) is a critic and curator based in Los Angeles. Her writing has appeared in *Aperture*, the *Architectural Review*, *Dezeen*, the *Los Angeles Times*, and *Wallpaper*. In 2018, she was a co-curator of the US Pavilion at the Venice Architecture Biennale.

Sandra Cattaneo Adorno

Ten Years

Venice Biennale - Palazzo Bembo
20 April - 24 November

Agenda
Exhibitions to See

Japanese Women Photographers

A much-needed counterpoint to the male-dominated canon of Japanese photography, *I'm So Happy You Are Here: Japanese Women Photographers from the 1950s to Now*, curated by Pauline Vermare, Mariko Takeuchi, and Lesley A. Martin, presents a wide range of photographic approaches, including installation-based work, video, and the printed page. Coinciding with a book published by Aperture, *I'm So Happy* provides an indispensable introduction to the contributions of Japanese women to photography, showcasing intimate observations of everyday life, critical perspectives on history, and radical experiments with the medium.

I'm So Happy You Are Here: Japanese Women Photographers from the 1950s to Now at Rencontres d'Arles, France, July 1–September 29, 2024

Mika Ninagawa, *Untitled*, 1998, from the series *17 9 '97*
Courtesy the artist

Akinbode Akinbiyi

When asked about his street photographs, Akinbode Akinbiyi once said: "I am looking for my childhood." For more than four decades, the British Nigerian photographer has chronicled life in cities across the world—Durban, Lagos, Brasília, Bamako—with a sensitive, poetic eye. *Being, Seeing, Wandering* is Akinbiyi's first solo exhibition in Germany, where he moved in the early 1990s and won this year's Hannah Höch Prize. The show brings together more than 120 photographs, highlighting Akinbiyi's enduring interest in the layered and improvisational character of cities he's visited and called home.

Akinbode Akinbiyi, from the series *Lagos, All Roads*, ca. 1980
© the artist and courtesy the Berlinische Galerie

Akinbode Akinbiyi: Being, Seeing, Wandering at the Berlinische Galerie, June 8–October 14, 2024

LaToya Ruby Frazier, *Sandra Gould Ford Wearing Her Work Jacket and Hard Hat in Her Meditation Room in Homewood, PA*, 2017
Courtesy Gladstone Gallery

LaToya Ruby Frazier

One of the great portrayers of twenty-first-century postindustrial American life, LaToya Ruby Frazier has covered stories from her hometown of Braddock, Pennsylvania, indelibly shaped by Carnegie Steel, to the water crisis in Flint, Michigan. "I've used my camera as a compass to direct a pathway toward the illuminated truth of the indomitable spirit of working-class families and communities," Frazier says. For her first major museum survey, the artist presents ten bodies of work that peerlessly narrate the potential of images to inspire radical solidarity.

LaToya Ruby Frazier: Monuments of Solidarity at the Museum of Modern Art, New York, May 12–September 7, 2024

Tropical Modernism

As former colonies in South Asia and West Africa gained independence from British rule in the mid-twentieth century, "tropical modernism"—an architectural style that mixed modernist ideals with local building traditions and materials—emerged as a key expression of political and administrative power. Heads of state in newly independent countries, Jawaharlal Nehru in India and Kwame Nkrumah in Ghana, for instance, commissioned major buildings in the style. *Tropical Modernism: Architecture and Independence* situates this approach against a background of anticolonial struggle and the flourishing of multifarious architectural modernisms across the world.

Tropical Modernism: Architecture and Independence at the Victoria and Albert Museum, London, March 2–September 22, 2024

Aditya Prakash, from *Photo Album of Architectural Projects, People, Landscapes and Aditya Prakash*, 1960–2000
© Aditya Prakash fonds, Canadian Centre for Architecture, Montreal

Timeline
A Brief History of the Moon

Jupiter has ninety-five moons. Earth, one. Judging from the number of photographs of our singular satellite, one might think there were more objects in our orbit. Silver moons have filled books, blogs, almanacs, and atlases for almost two hundred years. All are pictures of the same thing, yet each photograph of the moon is unique. The unchangeable subject highlights the medium's variability. Just as the moon reflects the sun's light, these pictures reflect back to us something about photography itself.
—**Kim Beil**

John W. Draper's daguerreotype is often erroneously described as the first photograph of the moon; in fact, it is only the earliest known surviving example. The historian Dan Streible has tracked down this image's many appearances—reversed, color corrected, misattributed—arguing that these copies derive from a daguerreotype likely made on March 26, 1840, from a rooftop observatory in New York.

Almost a century later, humans were finally able to photograph the surface of the moon itself, rather than a plaster doppelgänger. When the Apollo II lunar module landed on the moon on July 20, 1969, approximately 650 million people were watching live on television. Many of these viewers marked the occasion with snapshots. Photographs of the moon on TV brought our satellite down to Earth and into the familiar realm of the photo-album.

The engineer James Nasmyth and amateur astronomer James Carpenter were captivated by lunar geology. Believing that the moon's cratered surface resulted from volcanic activity, they set out to prove their theory. Since telescopic views were lacking in detail, Nasmyth and Carpenter created plaster models of the moon's surface and photographed them in raking light, adding the realism of photography to their miniature mock-ups. The results appeared in their 1874 publication *The Moon: Considered as a Planet, a World, and a Satellite*.

Astronomers' interest in photography was immediate, although it took several years to adapt existing telescopes to the cosmic task. Early issues included the difficulty of tracking the moon's movement through the sky during long exposures and focusing its dimly reflected light. In 1851, an ongoing collaboration between the Boston photographer John Adams Whipple and the Harvard College Observatory finally resulted in success. Their daguerreotypes were enlarged and copied for display at London's Great Exhibition.

The British photographer Warren De La Rue reported being so "charmed" by Whipple's lunar daguerreotypes that he set out to make his own images. Around 1858, De La Rue produced stereoscopic images by photographing the full moon at two different times of the year, allowing the moon's tilted elliptical orbit to create the variation required for the three-dimensional effect. Sir John Herschel likened De La Rue's stereo views to seeing the moon with a giant's eyes set thousands of miles apart.

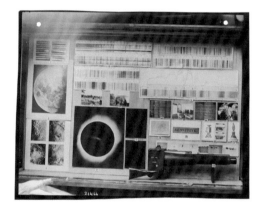

Thomas W. Smillie became the first official photographer of the Smithsonian in 1870 and its inaugural curator of photography in 1896. During his long tenure, he acquired photographs and photographic equipment, organized exhibitions, and documented the collections in a series of cyanotypes. Smillie noted his efforts to gather "material evidences" of photography's remarkable early achievements—his finds for the museum included astronomical photographs such as Lewis M. Rutherfurd's 1865 image of the moon, seen upside down in Smillie's 1913 cyanotype.

Kim Beil teaches art history at Stanford University. She is the author of *Good Pictures: A History of Popular Photography* (2020).

Viewfinder
In the 1960s, Akihiko Okamura photographed Northern Ireland with understated eloquence.

Declan Long

Early in the BBC documentary series *Once Upon a Time in Northern Ireland* (2023), a powerful collection of personal testimonies on the Troubles, one speaker recalls his childhood excitement during the first waves of civil unrest. "It was mad . . . it was like a movie," he reminisces, thinking back on the innocent elation he experienced as mass protests, running street battles, and military patrols became regular features of everyday life. Inevitably, as the daily drama intensified, with bombings, shootings, and funerals dominating the headlines, the desperate gravity of the situation became clear. Even to kids playing with pretend guns on the backstreets of Derry and Belfast, as the BBC interviewee remembers, "this was serious . . . it wasn't like a movie anymore."

The Japanese photographer Akihiko Okamura first visited Northern Ireland during this formative phase of the thirty-year conflict, and his images capture, with understated eloquence, a sense of reality as shifting and unstable, both not quite real and all too real. In 1968, Okamura moved to Dublin with his family, prompted by a plan to explore the Irish roots of President John F. Kennedy. From there he made numerous trips north of the border, documenting occasions of historic significance, such as landmark civil rights marches, while also attending to people and places on the margins of the era's main events.

Okamura was unfamiliar with the specific circumstances of Northern Ireland's political divisions but no stranger to societies upturned by warfare, struggle, and suffering. Before settling in Ireland, he had photographed the chaos and cruelty of the Vietnam War, gaining extraordinary access to Viet Cong camps, and traveled to Cambodia, Malaysia, and Korea, documenting life in nations coping with the corrosive, long-term effects of colonialism. (Later, he also reported on the Nigerian Civil War and journeyed through Ethiopia, photographing victims of famine.) Tracking political developments and, more routinely, everyday existence in Ireland during the late 1960s and early '70s, Okamura brought a worldly outsider's capacity to find surprising new angles, and the patience and sensitivity of someone willing to stick around, to look beyond the breaking news.

The pictures selected for Atelier EXB's publication *Akihiko Okamura: Les Souvenirs des autres* (The Memories of Others, 2024)

This page:
Preparations for
the Twelfth of July
celebrations in the
Fountain area, Derry
city, Northern Ireland,
ca. 1969

Opposite:
The Fountain area,
Derry city, Northern
Ireland, ca. 1969

and an associated exhibition at the Photo Museum Ireland, Dublin, showcase Okamura's subtly modulating stylistic range, combining moments of big-picture photojournalistic storytelling, gently surrealistic black comedy, and hazily dreamlike glimpses of communities or individuals in states of fearful transition or uneasy stasis. Some images have orthodox historical value. There are, for instance, valuable shots of key characters in early episodes of the Troubles. Okamura catches the stern vanity of the firebrand sectarian preacher Ian Paisley as he lays a wreath at the culmination of an Ulster Loyalist parade, his hair slicked and quiffed like a '50s rock-and-roll star. The civil rights activist Bernadette Devlin, Paisley's left-wing, nonsectarian rival for the most dynamic public speaker of the era, is memorably pictured in a typical pose: megaphone in hand, leading the action from a barricade during Derry's Battle of the Bogside in 1969. The most resonant of the photographs, however, are those with more unassuming, antiheroic attributes. They stir feelings of unusual intimacy with characters living through the strange convulsions of their times.

Okamura singles out low-key moments, discovering worlds within worlds. He seems to be, as W. G. Sebald once said of his fellow writer Robert Walser, a "clairvoyant of the small," looking for what we might learn of desire, sadness, loneliness, or dreaming among the dispersed, matter-of-fact materials of daily life. Two women clamber through a

This page:
Street memorial on
Lecky Road, Derry city,
Northern Ireland, ca.
1971; opposite: Women
crossing through British
Army barricade, Derry
city, Northern Ireland,
ca. 1969
© Estate of Akihiko
Okamura/Junko Sato

makeshift army barricade; one wears a bright red coat, its cheerful design an incidental affront to the surrounding gloom. Two little girls, prim and dainty in their Sunday best, pay their respects at an improvised memorial to a shooting victim on a Derry street. Behind the shadowy presence of an armed soldier in heavy fatigues, a pair of pristine white wedding dresses appear in the window of a bridal shop. Another lone figure, a young man in a slim-fitting suit, leans against a lamppost reading a newspaper; above him, street and shop signs declare "No Entry" and "Eclipse."

There are quite a few signs in Okamura's Irish oeuvre: street names, traffic directions, advertising posters. Here and there, the texts hint at hope of stable meaning—such as in one picture of a grieving woman carrying a protest banner, appealing for justice—or unbending allegiance to a political position: in another shot, showing residents gaily decorating a terraced street for the Unionist community's Twelfth of July celebrations, we see the intransigent slogan "No Surrender" emblazoned on a wall mural. Often, words produce moments

Okamura singles out low-key moments, discovering worlds within worlds.

of mischievous irony: a helmeted soldier, bearing a shield and a baton, framed partially by a sign saying "caterers"; or the words "Police Enquiries" posted outside a fortified Royal Ulster Constabulary station, barely visible on the ludicrously forbidding sheet metal facade. If with such teasing image-text contradictions Okamura gestured toward satire, he did so without becoming direct or dogmatic. However dark their humor, however bleak their mood, his photographs create space to see ordinary life at the time of the Troubles a little differently: one unexpected scene, one small detail, after another.

Declan Long is a critic
based in Dublin, where
he teaches at the National
College of Art and Design.

Studio Visit
Stefan Ruiz's Brooklyn home is a visual biography of his prolific career.

Brendan Embser

Stefan Ruiz and his home studio, Brooklyn, January 2024
Photographs by Steven Molina Contreras for *Aperture*

There's one townhouse on Bergen Street in the Boerum Hill neighborhood of Brooklyn that doesn't look like any of the others. Instead of traditional brownstone, a layer of cement, raked with tines into rhythmic grooves, covers the facade from the garden level to the roofline. The house belongs to the photographer Stefan Ruiz, and it's getting a makeover.

"Basically, most of the places have been fixed up at least once or twice," Ruiz told me when I visited last winter. "There are still a few people who have been here for fifty years or more. It's gotten way fancier."

Ruiz lives and works on the lower two floors and rents out the two apartments above. The downstairs contains his archive of magazines, negatives, and work prints. The cabinets are covered with an epic collage of clippings, serving as mood board and visual biography.

His living room and office, on the parlor floor, are densely packed with photographs, records, books, and objects of curiosity that represent his prolific collecting and constant travel.

On the walls are four vivacious portraits by Malick Sidibé that Ruiz bought from Sidibé's studio in Bamako, Mali. On his bookshelves are numerous hand-painted photo-sculptures from Mexico, freestanding silhouettes with bespoke wooden frames. He has masks from South Africa, a regiment of Pablo Escobar figurines, a portrait of Emiliano Zapata painted by a man incarcerated in California's Soledad prison, and religious art—"nuns in ecstasy," he calls them. "I went berserk collecting records too," Ruiz, who is also a DJ, said.

In 2002, after a decade of freelance work for *i-D* and breakthrough fashion campaigns for Caterpillar and Camper,

Ruiz landed a job as creative director of *Colors*, the brash culture magazine established by the Italian fashion label Benetton. "The fact that I got an actual job from *Colors* meant that I was able to get a loan," he explained. "Because I'd never had a job, like a steady paycheck." His mother's friend had a studio in Brooklyn, so he went to a small real-estate agency and looked at a few places in the area. "And then," he said, "I just did it." Ruiz has done a lot of restoration on the house himself, but not the "scratch coat," a stucco-concrete mix applied prior to the new brownstone top coat that will return the facade to landmark standards.

Restoration is a religion in Boerum Hill. The name itself, devised in the 1960s by newly arrived homeowners, was a salvage operation intended to demarcate several blocks south of downtown Brooklyn. Boerum Hill was an "audacious promise, or a bluff," the novelist Jonathan Lethem, who grew up in the neighborhood, has written. The arrival of artists and young white families gave banks the confidence to approve mortgages. But while rows of nineteenth-century brownstones were protected from demolition and steadily climbed in value, Black, Dominican, and Puerto Rican residents were displaced or excluded.

Ruiz has photographed celebrities and presidents, luxury travel locations in South America, and houses in the Hamptons, but he has more in common with Boerum Hill's first generation than the high-flying buyers of multimillion-dollar listings today.

In 1991, Ruiz was bartending at a hotel restaurant in San Francisco and teaching art at San Quentin State Prison. He had lived in West Africa for two years, working for an art historian. The novelist Alice Walker liked the pictures Ruiz had made there and gave him a small grant, which was just enough to buy a Hasselblad and other equipment an older photographer was looking to off-load. One day, he met a crew that was casting for a Levi's ad. This was the grunge era, and the brand wanted a diverse group in their catalog. Ruiz took nine pictures of his friends, which led to his assisting on a photoshoot for Levi's, and soon he was getting work for *i-D*: in Oakland he photographed street-fashion stories, and in London he made portraits of the editor Edward Enninful and the artist Steve McQueen. His first and only

Ruiz's disarmingly shy manner creates a sense of openness with his subjects, whether it's Bill Clinton or Bad Bunny.

i-D cover was of Sarah Cracknell, the lead singer of Saint Etienne.

"I never got paid for anything I did for *i-D*," Ruiz recalled. But he was hired for advertising campaigns. Often people couldn't quite place Ruiz, whose mother is Italian American and whose father's family is Mexican. "Some people thought I was French, some people thought I was Brazilian; they didn't know where I was from," he explained. Perhaps that ambiguity, and Ruiz's disarmingly shy manner, creates a sense of openness with his subjects, whether it's Bill Clinton or Bad Bunny.

By the end of the 1990s, he had begun working with Caterpillar on a street-wear campaign. For one ad, he photographed a young Mexican model named Victor, cast from a shopping mall, at a modernist Palm Springs gas station. The radiant lighting and self-possessed pose would become Ruiz's signature. "Maybe the photo makes you think about something," Ruiz has said of his work, in a Vice documentary. "Maybe it's not just eye candy. Not just a one-idea thing."

Ruiz used to have photoshoots in his house and lay out stories for editing. Now that he and his partner, Caroll Taveras,

have a young daughter, Lua, whose toys and books compete with Ruiz's own collections, space is at a premium. Yet the house on Bergen Street has allowed Ruiz to be an artist and a parent, and to avoid selling out—that very Gen X term.

"I've done photography for years. And I've figured out how to work it," Ruiz said. Renting the apartments upstairs helps him to break even and pursue the projects of his choosing. "I'm not making a profit. But I'm not really losing money either," he said. "Eventually, I'm gaining a house."

Brendan Embser is the senior editor of *Aperture*.

Curriculum
Alejandro Cartagena

A prolific photographer, editor, publisher, and champion of NFTs, Alejandro Cartagena has portrayed the often surreal consequences of importing the American dream across the Mexican border. He has photographed workers in truck beds from an overpass and offered tips for politicians taking selfies. For his decade-long chronicle on the effects of real-estate speculation in Monterrey, Mexico, where he lives and works, Cartagena produced a "For Dummies"–style guidebook complete with tips about choosing a good neighborhood.

MUNDO FELIZ
The album *Mundo Feliz* (1991), by Fobia, was the soundtrack of my skateboarding days. In retrospect, the lyrics feel like a high-school kid's poetry notebook, the scribbling of fantasies of freedom from parents, the building of a little world where love, politics, and real life don't exist. We all dreamed of a *mundo feliz* at age fifteen: "I won't lend it to anyone / And you won't be in it / I won't let you in / Into my happy world."

DISCARDED PHOTOGRAPHS
I started going to flea markets on the outskirts of Mexico City in the mid-2010s and became obsessed with the idea of collecting discarded objects, especially photographs. The ones I found had lost their original meaning and had become malleable, open to reinterpretation. I continue to collect and classify them. They are a source of understanding the structures with which we build collections of photographic images.

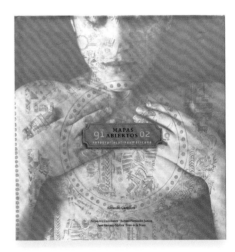

OPEN MAPS
In 2004, after taking a photography class where we analyzed photographs in ways I didn't even know you could, I quit my restaurant-manager job and volunteered at a photography center in Nuevo Leon, Mexico. I was part of the team putting together *Mapas Abiertos* (Open Maps), an exhibition that gave me an awareness of many Latin American photographers who were telling stories of our culture. Witnessing, for the first time, all those beautiful images that I related to emotionally, culturally, and conceptually was memorable.

DAVID HARVEY
To live in a place means having the opportunity to mold that place and to fight for your home. Until I read David Harvey's 2008 essay "The Right to the City," I passively experienced urban space with no understanding of the manifestations of power. I can pinpoint the start of my thirteen-year photography project about the city of Monterrey to discovering Harvey's ideas about how when we remake the city, the city remakes us.

BACK TO THE FUTURE
Growing up in the Dominican Repuclic, I saw this trilogy and wondered what the future might look like. I, too, desired to have adventures and time travel. Now, the films are conduits for telling stories to my kids about the 1980s, when I lived on a small island in the Caribbean and had silly dreams of a future with flying cars and hover boards.

EL SILENCIO
This is the best album by Caifanes, one of Mexico's most important 1990s rock bands. The songs' lyrics made no sense most of the time but that was just beautiful to experience as a teenager. I had little exposure to good rock music in Spanish, and with *El Silencio* (1992), I discovered a movement called *rock en tu idioma*, or "rock in your language." I always come back to this album. It is a safe place to feel that nothing matters.

Spotlight

Avion Pearce, winner of the 2024 Aperture Portfolio Prize, creates a world between reality and dreams.

Lucy McKeon

In her poem "A Litany for Survival," Audre Lorde speaks of the precarious experience of living with the knowledge that one's survival is not only not guaranteed but actively, purposefully threatened. Avion Pearce borrowed a line from Lorde for the title of their series *In the Hours Between Dawn* (2022–24), an ode to the possibilities of the midnight hours. The experience of the queer and trans community of color in Brooklyn that Pearce photographs is a testament to Lorde's words. Survival—half shrouded, yet insistent—can appear in forms both soft and strong.

Pearce, who works with 8-by-10 and medium-format cameras, considers how photography shapes ideas about identity and history. "I was looking at some of the tools that have been used to construct these ideas," Pearce told me recently, describing their desire to use older photographic methods to address the way the form has influenced how we see and understand the world. The presence of other photographic documents—a film still, a poster, a backdrop showing men in suits outside a Harlem jazz club—within Pearce's pictures is also notable, and seems to speak to the power, promise, and perils of imagery.

Merging analog techniques with political purpose and a poetic sensibility, Pearce creates a visual realm that operates somewhere between reality and dreams. How to express what goes purposefully unseen? The assault on trans and queer rights, recently emboldened in this country, requires new ways of thinking about visibility, Pearce said, describing a certain aesthetic associated with queer photography: subjects pictured in a straightforward and highly perceivable way. "That work is really important and necessary, but I also feel that, in this particular moment, it's important to think about whether or not visibility is necessary, and when it's harmful." For some images, Pearce photographed at

Page 26:
Tamara, Clinton Hill, 2023;
page 27: *Caravan*, Clinton
Hill, 2023

This page:
Ellington, Crown Heights,
2023; opposite: *Offerings,
Both Ways*, 2022

night, while in others, they used a day-for-night technique that approximates night, allowing for a selective exposure within the frame while leaving the rest in darkness.

Born in Flatbush, Brooklyn, to Guyanese parents, Pearce now lives in New Haven, Connecticut. Growing up, their parents took many family snapshots of Pearce and their brother, and the photographer remembers bringing their father's 35mm camera to middle school to make pictures of friends. World-building and an attraction to magical realism is an inheritance from their mother, who shared an interest in beauty, detail, and the cultivation of a space.

Pearce attended Parsons School of Design for photography, and commercial photography, then advertising, before pursuing an MFA at Yale. It was there that Pearce was inspired by Abelardo Morell's use of the camera obscura, which is deployed in one of Pearce's particularly striking images: a figure lies in a dark

The assault on trans and queer rights, recently emboldened in this country, requires new ways of thinking about visibility.

Pearce explores photography's potential to chart the interplay between time, the body, and Brooklyn's transformation.

bed, the Brooklyn skyline floating upside down on the wall above their head like a dream made visible. The camera obscura technique, employed for centuries by painters, recalls Pearce's impressionistic use of light and shadow, focus and atmosphere throughout their imagery. Other influences include Ming Smith, Roy DeCarava, and Graciela Iturbide—photographers who innovated with light, motion, and ambiance—and the films of Wong Kar-wai and Rainer Werner Fassbinder.

Pearce's series also tells a story of housing insecurity and displacement, with Brooklyn, and especially Crown Heights, a character in its own right. Exploring photography's potential to chart the interplay between time, the body, and the borough's transformation, Pearce's expression relies as much on feeling as on fact. *In the Hours Between Dawn* inhabits multiple registers, a document of what is and a vision of what could be.

As in Lorde's "A Litany for Survival," Pearce's sight stretches, "looking inward and outward / at once before and after / seeking a now that can breed / futures."

Beyond Lorde, there is a distinct literary quality to Pearce's photographs. "Toni Morrison has this really beautiful way of describing light, of describing atmosphere, of describing the mundane," said Pearce, who in a recent rereading of *Beloved* was particularly taken by Morrison's depiction of the pulsing red light that fills the house at 124 Bluestone Road, where the ghost of Beloved returns to her mother.

"I just really wanted to know how that could translate to the process of making an image," Pearce explained, considering how transcendent color might communicate feeling, sensation, even memory. "Is it possible," they added, "to transport someone to a space or a time using something like light and color?" The luminous imprint of *In the Hours Between Dawn* lingers long after one's eyes have left the artist's world.

Van, Shirley Chisholm Park, 2022

All photographs from the series *In the Hours Between Dawn*, 2022–24
Courtesy the artist

Lucy McKeon is a writer and editor based in New York.

Avion Pearce is the winner of the 2024 Aperture Portfolio Prize. A solo exhibition of their work will be presented at Baxter St at the Camera Club of New York in June 2024.

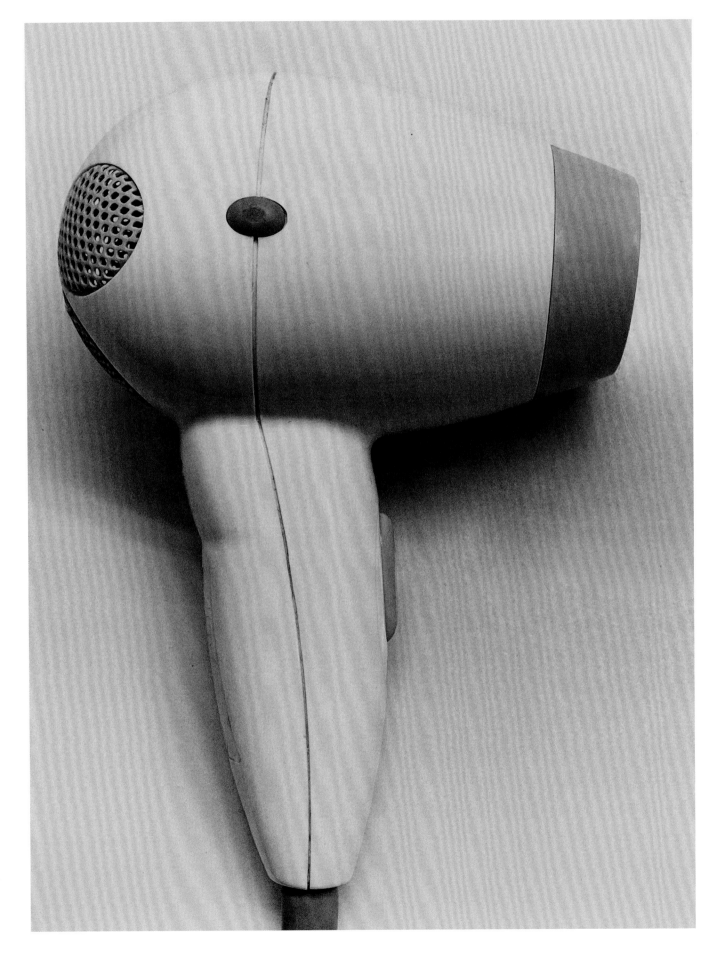

Paul Kooiker, *Untitled (Föhn)*, 2022
Courtesy the artist
(See page 132)

The Design Issue

Yes, that's right, this issue of *Aperture* is a little different. We've introduced some design changes to make the magazine slightly more inviting, easier to hold, to fit in your bag, to take and read on the go—or to sit with while you peruse at home. While the format may be different, the same editorial spirit drives this publication, running since 1952: a commitment to presenting a spectrum of ideas and photography, from past and present, reproduced with care and thoughtfully considered through engaging, approachable writing. We live in a strange, beguiling, sometimes uneasy but always evolving world of images. We hope to help make sense of it all.

Aperture's design has shifted numerous times over the past seven decades. The very first issue was a modest 6 ¼ by 9 ⅜ inches. We are fortunate to have a rich history from which to draw inspiration and direction. Our design team of Scott Williams and Henrik Kubel at A2/SW/HK, London, took a deep dive into the archive in search of *Aperture*'s design DNA, assessing everything from combinations of classic serif and modernist sans serif typefaces, text layout, image placement, and, of course, our logo, which remains true to the original, just centered and more prominently placed on the magazine's front cover.

While reflecting on our own design history, we were reminded of how the experience of looking at photographs is so often enlivened by the work of visionary graphic, digital, or exhibition designers. The history of photography has been defined by brilliant collaborations across disciplines. In these pages, we see connections between fashion, industrial design, and architecture, and the ways photography can envision a response to urgent social and environmental challenges. If photography helps frame the world, design plays an essential role in framing photography.

Duro Olowu Cutting a Figure

The former lawyer turned designer Duro Olowu creates fashion moments on a resolutely human scale. Born in Lagos into a Nigerian Jamaican family, Olowu had a cosmopolitan upbringing, traveling to Europe and absorbing cultural influences ranging from album covers to Yves Saint Laurent. His tenacious curiosity, like his patternmaking, seems limitless—and his deep knowledge of photography has informed his fashion line.

Instead of flashy runway shows, Olowu prefers private viewings that allow him to discuss his patchwork dresses and jacquard coats with the coterie of cultural figures who wear his richly patterned designs. Like him, they appreciate clothes in a context that celebrates collecting antiques, paintings, and handicrafts over any proximity to trends or celebrity endorsements. Olowu has also curated exhibitions in New York, London, and Chicago. On each occasion, he staged a vibrant dialogue, juxtaposing photography and painting, or West African heritage textiles and the innovative fabric creations of contemporary sculptors.

The editor Dan Thawley recently spoke with Olowu from his studio in Mason's Yard, in London. Olowu claims to have been a reluctant curator at first. Soon, however, he sensed a freedom in making exhibitions, the freedom to think about photography and fashion across genres and decades. The results offer a new way of seeing.

Dan Thawley: **Duro, there are some things I am curious to ask you about your relationship with photography. I wanted to start with collecting.**

Duro Olowu: I always shy away from the word *collect*. But I have quite a lot of photography, just because it was always a lot more accessible. In the 1990s and even up until the mid-2000s you could come across something one had always wanted, like an early Samuel Fosso or a Luigi Ghirri. Back then a lot of photography was just not recognized or put in the same category as fine art.

DT: **What is your relationship to photography as a fashion designer? The image of clothing is something you need to continue to produce, but it's also something that I can imagine is a powerful tool to inspire your creativity as well.**

DO: There are two aspects to that. There's a side of fashion photography which is very commercial, and then, of course, there's contemporary art and photography

in that realm. There's overlap. The relationship between design and fashion and other kinds of creativity has always been there since the 1920s and '30s, and in the work of a lot of photographers that I look at now—Peter Hujar, Kwame Brathwaite, Cindy Sherman, Anthony Barboza—people whose work I find as important as, say, Man Ray. I think it's a subconscious thing.

For designers, you can only tell if you have succeeded when you look at a photograph of someone dressed in your clothes, and they look very comfortable and confident—almost as though the clothes have become their armor, their shield. With great photographers, I always found that this was what they were able to do. Claude Cahun used clothing, objects, jewelry, and costume to empower herself as a very early pioneer of self-portraiture in photography and queer art. When you look at Malick Sidibé or Seydou Keïta or Carrie Mae Weems, you realize that they are using clothes as a language. So, as a designer, that is the language that I try to write with.

Clothing to me is not about fashion or trends. I'm designing for people that are interested in the culture of style, and people who want to use what I design to place themselves in the world in a certain way. For something to look modern and for something not to date or age, it has to reflect the times. I think great photography always reflects the present as much as the past. And in designing, that's what I try to do with clothing—not to replicate. It's my point of view. It's not an attempt to replicate what's in photographs. It's more an attempt to emulate the power of the gesture of photographs.

DT: **Does the way that a photograph freezes a silhouette—perhaps a drape in movement—ever stimulate you to replicate that gesture?**

DO: A great photograph—whether it's a still life or a portrait or some other kind of composition—is never forced. A great artist knows not just when to click but when the subject and mise-en-scène is just right enough to capture. Clothed or nude, it's incredibly emotional and powerful.

Fashion or clothing needs to emote, but it shouldn't be nostalgic. What changes over time are emotions, how people express themselves. That's what you see in great collections of clothing. If you looked at Madeleine Vionnet then, if you looked at certain things at a certain time, thirty years ago, for example, they probably didn't seem so radical. Or Sonia Delaunay, or even Patrick Kelly. Today, they appear even more radical than one can imagine.

I think great photography is like that. Which is why, in looking at contemporary photographers, whether it's Ming Smith or Dawoud Bey, one needs to also be open to the incredible power, savoir faire, and freedom that the history of photography has made possible in the art world. Many great photographers either started as photojournalists or made commercial work, like Madame Yevonde or Eve Arnold. So, I think photography is a very sinuous reference that is not bound by trends. I feel very lucky that I can look at Steven Meisel, who I consider to be one of the greatest fashion photographers ever, or Irving Penn or Clifford Coffin, in the same way I look at James Van Der Zee, Walker Evans, Mama Casset, or Tina Modotti.

Yto Barrada, *Fille en rouge jouant aux osselets* (Girl in Red – Playing Jacks), 1999
Courtesy the artist

I think photography is a very sinuous reference that is not bound by trends.

DT: **I've always appreciated how you spotlight portraiture on your social media. You post photographs of Black luminaries, amongst other fantastic images. How does that research establish your frame of cultural references when designing?**

DO: There's a kind of portraiture that involves a whole setup as a souvenir, and then there's the kind of portraiture made by artists, which I find really powerful, particularly when it's self-portraiture. Because there are two things at work. There's the element of exposing oneself, but also that of not exposing too much of oneself, because you have many more years and a lot more ideas that you want to pursue. I approach design questions in the same way.

Sometimes people can go through periods of their lives not being able to put a face to a writer or an artist. Look at Dawoud Bey's portrait of David Hammons. When you look at these portraits, they are sort of an eye into the reasoning behind Hammons's work. When one looks at the artist Lee Miller in Man

Ray's photographs, you are not looking at what you imagine to be the personality of the subject. You're actually looking at what the person does in the real world, because that's what emerges. The human body is restless. The human mind is laden. You never know what you're going to get. When I see something that really emotes in that way, I'm always very conscious of how important it is in the context of contemporary art. Placed alongside portraiture in other mediums like painting or sculpture, it's very important to have the element of the photographic print.

DT: **You've curated some great shows, including *Making & Unmaking* at the Camden Art Centre in London in 2016 and *Seeing Chicago* at the Museum of Contemporary Art Chicago four years later. How do you go about manifesting your passion for photography in these projects?**

DO: I feel that what I do curatorially is a very important part of my whole oeuvre. I see it as an extension of what I do, and in the institutional shows I've done, the amount of photography is a testament to what we're talking about. To have Henri

Matisse and David Hammons and Brice Marden next to Dawoud Bey was something that, even curatorially, I know a lot of the people, when I was putting the show together, couldn't understand until they walked into the room.

I consider photographers to be artists and artists to be photographers. I never think: Oh, do I have to create a special section for photography? I'm actually very anti that. I'm not saying museums shouldn't have a Diane Arbus show, a Gordon Parks show, a Malick Sidibé show. I'm not saying that they shouldn't have their own rooms. But I'm always surprised when the institutional shows that are not solo shows hardly ever include photography. Because I think it's such a natural thing to include. That's obviously changing a lot. You see a lot more of that now.

In looking at a body of work, say, in the '80s, how could I look at David Wojnarowicz and not see Peter Hujar? How could I look at artists like Carrie Mae Weems even, and not think of Kara Walker's work? It's very different work, but it's just as emotive: powerful stories of women of color, emoting how they feel, not just about themselves but how they've been thought of for centuries. The same way I look at Eve Arnold's photographs. I feel that the way she captured the model in Harlem, the way she even captured Marilyn Monroe, came from

I always feel it's important for any show I curate to reflect this deep conversation amongst all the mediums.

who she was as a woman, being able to understand what the camera needed to pull out of that. I couldn't look at that sort of work and think it had to be in a separate section. I could only think of that work in relation to or mixed up with other things.

It's not such a new idea. I mean, Surrealists did that. You had Man Ray and Claude Cahun mixed up with Jean Arp and Hannah Höch, and the other Dadaists. It wasn't unusual up until I think the '60s, when a different kind of mindset came in. That's changing, or that's practically changed now. And I always feel it's important for any show I curate to reflect this deep conversation between all the mediums that continue to exist amongst artists in real life.

DT: **We all consume so many images on-screen now. But the object of the photograph is such a dynamic thing as well. What do you appreciate about the printed medium, and how it has changed over time?**

DO: It's very interesting you bring that up. The first real contact we have with

anything that will later sort of place itself in our lives as art is with photographs and prints. As a child, you look at a magazine or you look at a postcard or you're handed a photograph. Even practically as a baby, you are often first shown what you look like in a photograph of yourself. Later, as you go from childhood into adulthood, magazines, books, and other visual materials are filled with photographs that define your identity.

I have so much awe and respect for the use of a nondigital camera, the labor and development of film, preferably with no retouching. In looking at the photograph as an object, you're almost doing so as you would look at a 1920s Paul Poiret dress, Yves Saint Laurent haute couture jacket from the '70s, or an embroidered midcentury Yoruba agbada robe. You're looking at how it was made in the same way you look at the fabrication and finish of beautiful garments. So that when you come across it in a museum or gallery, you recognize that it is also powerful, beautiful, and important because of how it was made. *Making & Unmaking* was all about that human effort. The hand in the work.

DT: **We would never know much about certain art practices and movements from the twentieth century if it weren't for people like Ugo Mulas taking photographs of Lucio Fontana, and all of the Arte Povera artists. Photography reveals relationships and communities. And records from previous generations are so incredibly precious for that very reason.**

DO: Of course. Once again, the Dawoud Bey photographs of David Hammons with the snowballs. If that hadn't been

documented, how would we know that those snowballs melted—and the political and social commentary therein?

DT: **How have your interactions with cultural institutions informed your interest in and knowledge about photography?**

DO: Finding great photography in museums, by both known and unknown artists, is exhilarating and inspiring. The Metropolitan Museum of Art, the International Center of Photography,

and the Studio Museum in Harlem have exceptional examples in their collections, as does the Art Institute of Chicago. When I'm in Paris, I always visit the Jeu de Paume. The Fondation Cartier presented the first really incredible museum-worthy show of an African artist in the photography world—that was Seydou Keïta's show there in 1994. It was a beginning in many ways for how work by an artist from the continent was perceived and exhibited abroad.

I recently saw—and was blown away by—the artist Lisetta Carmi's show at the Estorick Collection, a small museum in London for twentieth-century Italian art. I have to also mention people like Rotimi Fani-Kayode, who I love, whose work I've known for thirty years, and who only now is being recognized. Because of the current possibilities for queer artists, photographers, painters, his work is being revisited and being shown in a very different way. But my favorite is the Photographers' Gallery in London, a small but renowned museum that I've visited since my teens. It exposed me to the most amazing group of inspiring international artists working in this medium, many of whom have informed my fashion collections and curatorial projects.

DT: **You touched upon the role of color earlier. Do you ever operate as a colorist, looking at photography when you put together your patterns and your different swatches and fabrics that you've created for your fashion line?**

DO: Absolutely. I have to say that it's photography and film, and photography is really important. It's the Technicolor aspect of everything—a kind of faded Technicolor. It's not jarring. When I design textiles, even if they're monotone, even if they're in very vivid colors, the whole idea is that it's not jarring. It doesn't make your eyes ache. Because it has to be easy on the eye—and on the

This page:
Duro Olowu's boutique in Mason's Yard, London, 2019; opposite: A look from Olowu's fall/winter 2014 collection.
Photograph by Luis Monteiro
Courtesy Duro Olowu

heart. It's a very emotional thing. So people like Joel Meyerowitz, I love.

Like Gordon Parks, I love the way William Eggleston can transform a painful photograph—a clear display of segregation or racism—into an empowering one for the person segregated against because they're wearing the most beautiful, simple clothing in the most vivid color. It's a very conscious effort, I think, on the part of the artist. It helps me see how color looks to other people, how color is represented.

I learned very early that after I've designed a fabric and I've seen the first swatches, when I do the variations or we cut the outfits, I put the different looks together and shoot them. When I see the photographs, I have to say they look like what I designed, but the intensity of the color is a hundred times more. It's a very empowering, exciting thing. Sometimes it's black and red or yellow and blue. It's not necessarily a whole cacophony of print. It could be solid colors, but when you see the luminosity, it reminds me of Luigi Ghirri's photographs of a veranda, or an umbrella on the seaside, or of a curtain in the front of a mechanic's shop. When you see your work photographed, you realize how the photograph has made it real to you.

If you really look at a photograph by an artist, there's something about the way they try to manipulate the color, even if it's black and white. There's Barkley L. Hendricks's photographs. He's one of the greatest painters ever. But he was also an incredible photographer. There's a picture of the two women at the airport in mink coats, but also a man in Nigeria in 1978. Hendricks happened to go to FESTAC, the Nigerian arts festival. He just stopped this guy in that fuchsia top and trousers and photographed him. Now, if you look at that fuchsia, I don't care whether you work with the best silk-dyeing mill, you never imagine that you can get that color. And then, when you look at it in the photograph, I think that is exactly the future that I want. It really helps me see fashion as more than just something flat.

DT: **Do you take many photos yourself?**

DO: Well, most of the pictures I put on Instagram that aren't credited to someone else, they're my photos. It's not something that I've ever thought I want

to pursue as an art. I love taking photos because when I'm taking them, I'm not thinking. I'm just capturing that moment. All my photos on the streets of New York, Dakar, whatever, when I look at them later, I realize I wasn't as familiar with certain things. That's why I respect photographers. Because after a while, they somehow manage to sense what's going on completely in that frame, before they take the picture. Nothing is really left to chance.

Dan Thawley is an editor, curator, and creative director based in Paris.

David Hartt

In his photographs, films, and installations, Hartt reveals the intersections between architecture and history.

Mimi Zeiger

Paradise Lost

More people moving out.
This place is dead.

Previous spread:
A Colored Garden (detail),
2022. Tapestry mounted
to linen

This spread:
Stills from *Adrift*, 2015.
16 mm film. 7 minutes,
44 seconds, color, sound

Hartt's nuanced approach to addressing identity and colonial history is evident in his way of thinking about images.

TUVALU IS SINKING. In a few decades, the island nation in the South Pacific might be mostly waves. Many of us know this from the internet, the island's submersion a de facto symbol of climate change, much like starving polar bears stranded on floating icebergs. The artist David Hartt knows about Tuvalu because he went there in 2015 to make a film called *Adrift* and to witness firsthand the effects of rising sea levels. He's traveled to swamplands in Florida and to Jamaica, where the artist Frederic Church sketched plein air studies. And he found the exact location in Ohio where the landscape painter Robert Duncanson set his easel for *Blue Hole, Flood Waters, Little Miami River* (1851). For more than a decade, he's made artworks—photographs, essayistic films, sculptural and sound installations—that examine place and history.

Visiting these diverse, far-flung locations isn't about ecotourism or metaphorical trophy hunting. Hartt's research-driven art leads him to crossroads where colonial-inflected landscapes meet rapidly changing environmental and political conditions. He weaves together interconnecting, unsettled narratives, drawing viewers into a delicate web that only appears fragile. "One mode of working is trying to engage in dimensionalized problems that I see as being fundamentally unstable," he told me recently.

Hartt lives in Philadelphia and teaches at the University of Pennsylvania. But he spent much of last fall traveling the globe, tracing these connections: an exhibition in Germany, a residency in France, new work made in South Africa. He studied art in Canada, where he was born, receiving a BFA from the University of Ottawa, followed by an MFA from the School of the Art Institute of Chicago, in the mid-1990s. And then he drifted away from art making—in that way one does when young and trying to figure out where life might lead. He worked as an intern in the photography department at the Art Institute of Chicago, whose curators Sylvia Wolf and Madeleine

Remember, after the Americans left,
they tried to get us to move here.

Grynsztejn made a huge impact on him, before leaving the field for more commercial pursuits in design and tech. He returned to art in earnest around 2009, showing at the Museum of Contemporary Art Chicago in 2013, and then exponentially: the Studio Museum in Harlem, the Museum of Modern Art, the Whitney Museum of American Art.

For some, a gap in the CV would cast a pall over their artistic trajectory, but not for Hartt. The time away allowed for culture to catch up with his ambitious and conceptually complex vision, which often uses archival research to illuminate present-day states of marginalization or displacement. He describes himself as grappling with his curiosity around places or events entangled in conditions of globalization or the Anthropocene. "David has this terrific understanding that disparate parts of the world get connected not in straight lines but in sort of discontinuous dotted lines, or circular formations, or indirectly ricocheting and ping-ponging off other parts of the world," Matthew S. Witkovsky, chair and curator of photography at the Art Institute of Chicago, told me.

Hartt was raised in Toronto, an adopted, biracial child of white, Jewish parents. His birth mother is white and his birth father was from the Caribbean. "I don't like the idea of cutting off the hyphenated nature of who I am," said Hartt. Indeed, there is a sense that this "hyphenated nature" shaped an ability to keenly understand his own perspective within a greater context. "I was the only Black kid at a high school of almost 1,500, 2,000 people," he added.

Hartt's nuanced approach to addressing identity and colonial history is evident in his way of thinking about images, architecture, and landscapes. "What I find interesting about his work," said the architecture historian Mabel O. Wilson, "is the way in which he makes you conscious that what you're looking at is a representation—you're not looking at the plant, you're looking at the image of the plant. And I think Blackness

is a construction. It's a mode of representation. And that is very useful in trying to understand the kinds of modalities that are possible."

The Histories (Le Mancenillier) captures Hartt's hyphenated identity in the most literal form. The site-specific multimedia artwork was installed, in 2019, at Beth Sholom Synagogue in suburban Philadelphia, a structure designed by Frank Lloyd Wright in 1954. A glazed, ziggurat-shaped roof tops Beth Sholom's main sanctuary, and, like in many of Wright's buildings, it leaks, producing a hothouse atmosphere. Hartt placed potted *Phalaenopsis* orchids—the magenta-and-white variety seen in supermarkets and known as moth orchids—within the space to capture drips. "We were trying to figure out how to make these sensitive interventions that wouldn't disrupt the day-to-day functioning of the synagogue but would reframe, or renegotiate, the audience's and the congregation's understanding of the space," explained Cole Akers, who organized the Beth Sholom exhibition and is a curator for the Glass House, the architect Philip Johnson's historic building and estate in New Canaan, Connecticut, that is now a museum. In 2021, Akers also invited Hartt to create *A Colored Garden*, a living intervention based on the still life paintings of Charles Ethan Porter, one of the only Black artists to attend the National Academy of Design.

The Histories (Le Mancenillier) interweaves tropical plants, photographic tapestries, Wright's architecture, and video footage of Haiti and Louisiana to produce a meditation on human and nonhuman migrations. The parenthetical part of the title comes from an 1851 composition by the pianist Louis Moreau Gottschalk that blends Creole and classical music; the name also refers to a type of swamp-loving tree. Hartt asked the Ethiopian pianist Girma Yifrashewa to reinterpret and record the music, which was then performed at Beth Sholom. (A recording also plays in the sanctuary.) The more one engages

Plants track through much of Hartt's recent output as a kind of meditation on what we think of as natural.

with Hartt's *The Histories (Le Mancenillier)*, the more its layers and complexities rise to the surface. Implications, too. His moth orchid tapestry—the lascivious houseplant presented sideways, devoid of background, and larger-than-life—seems to dare viewers to disconnect it from extractive global trade.

Plants, often in relation to architecture, track through much of Hartt's recent output as a kind of meditation on how what we think of as natural, such as a landscape or garden, is a human construct of sometimes visible, sometimes invisible structures. Plants also reflect a diasporic condition, specimens taken from one place, one habitat, and propagated in foreign lands. Hartt shares an old joke by the comedian Steven Wright to try to describe what he means by "garden," the title of a trio of artworks made over the last few years. He told it with the comedian's signature deadpan timing: "'You know,' he says, 'I have the world's largest seashell collection; I keep it scattered on beaches.' The joke is quite literal in that the garden, as I'm describing it, is a kind of dispersed diasporic, kind of global, domain."

The garden was the subject of Hartt's solo exhibition *Naturphilosophie*, which opened at Galerie Thomas Schulte, in Berlin, last November. On view was a suite of tapestries (with imagery translated from photographs) and photogravures that correlate to the work of the eighteenth-century Swedish botanist Carl Linnaeus. Hartt visited several cities in Europe, including Leiden, Uppsala, and Göttingen, that are associated with Linnaeus's contributions to the binomial nomenclature system—genus, species—for organisms. The system, designed to bring order to the natural world, can also be seen as an

instrument of control and extraction of what might have been called wild.

The *Garden* series is a way of making sense of a lost Eden—a prelapsarian fantasy of a world where nature exists beyond the built environment. Hartt's images purposefully border on an aesthetic he calls "cheesy sentimentality," a phrase used to both cite the work of the German Romantic printmakers he's inspired by and address the self-consciousness of photographic representation. In his drawing attention to a heightened reality, darker narratives come through. "One thing that my work has always dealt with is relationships between utopic realities and dystopic realities," Hartt said. "And so, in some ways, I'm trying to assemble, for lack of a better word, a kind of utopia through this articulation of multiple landscapes."

Connecting these geographies, *The Garden* series uses photographs to bridge past and present. But it would be wrong to constrain Hartt solely to photography. Like his explorations, his medium is interdisciplinary. "It's convenient, or at least common, to say in the last quarter century or so that the artist works across media," Witkovsky said. "He works across domains, really." For an exhibition on Pan-Africanism slated for November 2024, Witkovsky commissioned the film Hartt's been making in South Africa. "For David, architecture is important," Witkovsky explained. "Film is obviously important, since he makes them, and various photographic processes like photogravure, gelatin silver, colored prints. And then tapestry is exciting to him as design, or applied arts."

Referencing early photography in the nineteenth century, Hartt said, "I'm interested in photography as a kind of tool of analysis." At that time, the camera was less in the service of

an aesthetic practice and more a means of documentation for disciplines such as archaeology, anthropology, and cartography. Those scientific fields, of course, are inextricably linked with settlement and territorial expansion. Photography, in capturing images of exotic lands and bringing them back home, is complicit in these acts of dominion.

Hartt's working methods are exacting. When traveling he brings with him a large folder of images—photographs, paintings, prints—that prefigure his own framing. His South Africa film, titled *The Garden* (2024), was photographed in and outside Cape Town using a combination of time-lapse footage and bursts of still images to capture this incredibly biodiverse region. "It's an attempt for me to demonstrate 'plant-time,'" Hartt said in an email, sharing a link to an early cut of the film. In it, there is an overwhelming sense of motion and stillness, followed by isolation and decay. This is a place where European settlers poached flora, shipping it overseas, and introduced depleting monocultures. The film begins in the mountains and travels across the terrain, cutting through the city's suburban sprawl before reaching the port and, lastly, the shore. There's an uncanny familiarity to the fauna. "Many endemic species have been exported to compatible regions around the globe," he added. "California and the Mediterranean being two such areas."

In Hartt's frame, clouds race overhead as branches of low brush and agave lightly tremble. The gentle curvature of what appears to be a man-made reservoir mirrors the arch of a fern's fiddlehead. His camera zeroes in on the devastation of an uprooted gum tree in the middle of the city and the withering bloom of a bird-of-paradise. The film will have audio by the

sound artist Chris Watson, best known as a member of the electronic group Cabaret Voltaire. In his years as the popular naturalist David Attenborough's field recordist, Watson made nature recordings of the area.

For Hartt, hewing closely to the research is not limiting but rather about developing a set of artistic permissions. The art exists between parameter and liberation. "When I'm actually in the field, I no longer feel the burden of meaning, I already know what the work is going to mean," he stated. "Then I can really be present and engage with the site in a way that is all about looking through the camera, playing with depth of field, playing with composition, playing with POV, playing with exposure times. It is deeply physical and mental to be in that moment making images, and making a lot of images." For every thousand images he makes, only a small fraction—as few as three—become artwork. Those that do are freighted with meaning.

For all its antique references, Hartt's approach isn't an exercise in revisiting the past. He asks viewers to question, reinterpret, and speculate on what's possible. To make his art, to make it resonate as urgent, it is necessary to translate research into an embodied practice. Film and photography are, of course, a way of seeing, but in Hartt's artistic production, importantly, they require presence on the part of the artist and his audience. "Travel is not an indulgence; it is essential in terms of placing myself in relation to a historical context and recognizing how things have changed," he said. "Being in that moment, in that place, is critical."

Mimi Zeiger is a critic and curator based in Los Angeles.

This page:
From the cycle *The
Garden*, 2022-23;
opposite: *The Garden
(Rosa hybrida & Wisteria
sinensis / Tivoli, Italy /
May 19, 2022)*, 2022.
Installation view at
the Cincinnati Art
Museum, 2022.
Photograph by Rob
Deslongchamps
Courtesy the artist,
Corbett vs. Dempsey,
David Nolan Gallery, and
Galerie Thomas Schulte

An artist who saw photography as a means to restore his sense of wonder, Ghirri embraced a commission for the legendary carmaker.

Ferrari LUIGI GHIRRI

Michael Famighetti

Luigi Ghirri did not preoccupy himself with cars, but he did enjoy driving. He owned a number of Volkswagen Beetles that were constantly breaking down. In the 1980s, he switched to a Volvo station wagon, paragon of Swedish vehicular functionality and safety. An accumulation of unpaid traffic fines suggests he may not have been a great driver, or that he was blasé about traffic rules. Nonetheless, he crisscrossed Italy and Europe taking the photographs for which he is now celebrated: unpeopled landscapes that rush toward a vanishing point, architectural details, found images within images pasted around a town. All are realized in soft washes of warm color that cushion reality, making it feel ever so distant and dreamlike. Adele Ghirri, his daughter, who now manages his estate and archive from his former home and studio in Reggio Emilia, recalls that her father's cars were unwashed, neglected. His focus, one can assume, was on looking out the window for pictures. As Ghirri wrote, he sought to "observe the outside world in order to represent it."

For anyone growing up in and around Reggio, the mythic car manufacturer Ferrari, based in nearby Maranello, loomed large. The company, in a crowded field of contenders, is an apex of Italian style, industrial design, and brilliant ingenuity. Michael Mann's recent film *Ferrari* dramatizes the origins of the firm and the personal travails of its founder, Enzo Ferrari. Even so, on-screen, the cherry-red cars throbbing along twisting roads emerge as the indefatigable protagonists.

In the mid-1980s, Ghirri was invited to photograph at the Ferrari factory. The pictures feel like a laboratory record. Workers don elegant lab coats emblazoned with the company logo—that rearing horse. Interior leather samples are arranged in Ellsworth Kelly–like compositions. There is little sense of mechanical noise or grease. Even an image of molten steel being poured is quiet. By contrast, Chris Killip's noirish pictures from the Pirelli tire factory, stylish as they are, and made around the same time, hint at noisier manufacturing underway. Ghirri's Ferrari images haven't been widely published or exhibited. Not made for the public, they were used in a promotional publication, designed by the influential architect Pierluigi Cerri, that also included photographs by Walter Iscra, Gianni Rogliatti, Wolfgang Wilhelm, and a selection from the Ferrari archives.

Ghirri's photographs for Ferrari bring the company down to earth from the upper stratosphere of luxury.

Ghirri's interest in clean lines, perspective, and landscape can be traced back to his earlier job as a land surveyor. He was passionate about architecture and design, reading—and sometimes collaborating with—magazines such as *Ottagono*, *Lotus*, and *Domus*. He photographed many buildings by Aldo Rossi, an architect Ghirri admired for how the colors of his exteriors resonated with their surroundings. Like most photographers scratching out a living, Ghirri worked on commission from time to time, often merging image making with a story about design. In the 1980s the jewelry brand Bulgari hired him to take photographs of its newly minted Fifth Avenue store in New York. From 1975 to 1985, he worked with Marazzi, an Italian heritage tile company, using the opportunity of a commercial commission to create exquisite images of trompe l'oeil play and clever meditations on the act of picture making itself. The simple colored tiles presented a stage on which to work and arrange miniatures of a camera on a tripod, a baby grand piano, or, in a nod to Fra Angelico, an egg resting in a stand. A recently published book of Ghirri's work, *Italia in Miniatura* (2024), explores his interest in the detailed facsimiles of famous sites and landscapes at a theme park in Rimini. Ghirri's writings—his essays are prolific—ruminate on representations that shrink reality: postcards, atlases, Lilliputian worlds.

In the Ferrari images, too, there is a sense of making things small. As with his famous picture taken through a window at Versailles, deflating the ostentatious grandeur of the palace gardens, Ghirri's photographs for Ferrari bring the company down to earth from the upper stratosphere of luxury. This is seen on the factory floor and in a 1990 photoshoot staged on a hilltop overlooking Florence. A group of cars selected to celebrate the company's history was displayed and framed in an installation of cubes designed by Cerri. The Duomo is visible in the background. The cars look like toys. Describing the experience of being inside a Rossi building, Ghirri wrote: "There is also a joyous sense of wandering, magically, inside a wonderful toy, getting lost and finding one's way amid the gears and little wheels." The same might be said of his pictures for Ferrari. The pleasure of design is fully on display, and the glitz of a storied brand takes a backseat to a careful study of its component parts.

Michael Famighetti is the editor in chief of *Aperture*.

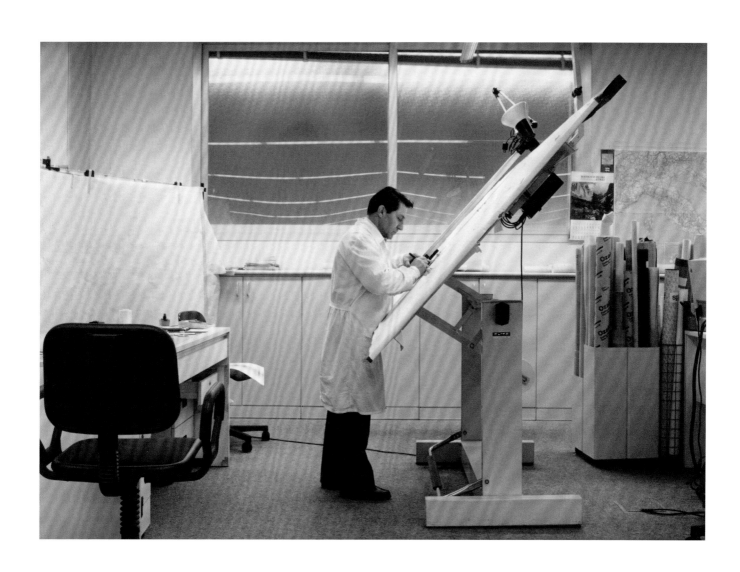

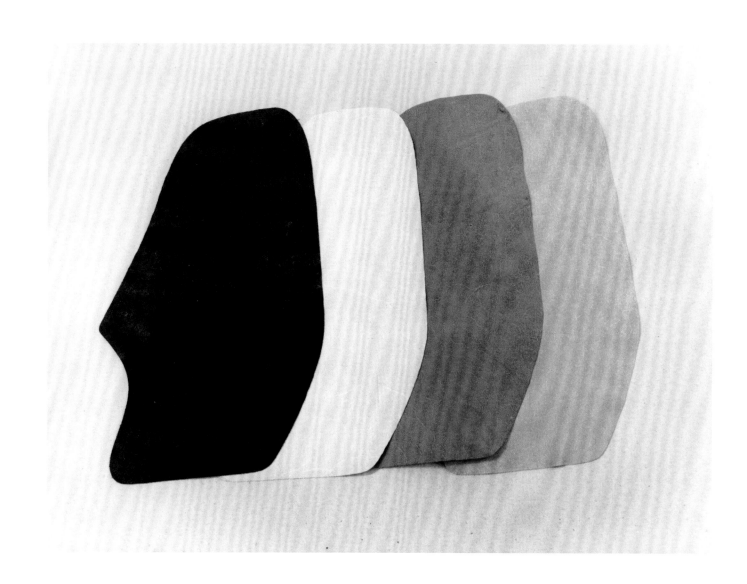

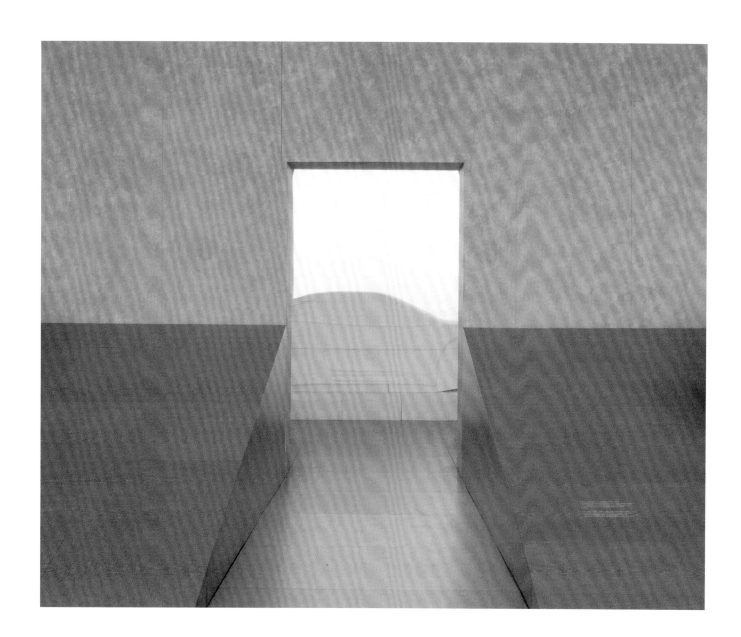

THE DESIGN ISSUE

Dayanita Singh
Better Living

Architecture and photography have always been intimately connected. These media share a few fundamentals: impacts of light and air, the balance of surface and depth, interiority and exteriority, and how these relations are mediated by the human body. Attending to such concerns has guided the expansive, fluid artistic practice of Dayanita Singh, whose open-ended approach to the photographic image has led to distinctive architectural modes of display. Encased in teak frames, screens, and boxes that often double as display cases which can be placed on walls and bookshelves, Singh's photographs circulate in modular forms that are adjustable to individual taste. They underscore how images accrue meaning over time, as people live and grow alongside them.

"To me, a photograph is something you touch and you move and it warps and it gets dented: it's alive," Singh remarked in a recent interview. Recounting her upbringing in India, she notes how her family's many photographs extended beyond stuffed albums and were wedged under the glass tabletop in their living space, where they seemed to vibrate with their own physicality, like another form of furniture. Her long-term engagement with the architects Geoffrey Bawa and Bijoy Jain draws from this personal history and aligns with a longer arc of modernist photography and its fascination with portraying surface, depth, and environment to extend the capacity of human vision. In her corpus of photographs made in conversation with Bawa's and Jain's respective designs, Singh's ever-curious photographic eye reveals shared principles between the two architects—commitment to the use of local materials, respect for craftspeople and traditions, seamless integration with the surrounding environment—while allowing their practices to remain fully distinct.

Born in 1919 in colonial Ceylon, Geoffrey Bawa traveled extensively throughout the United States, Asia, and Europe in the years after World War II before returning home, where he purchased a former rubber plantation in the southern coastal town of Bentota. He hoped to turn it into a garden villa like the ones he had seen in Italy. Realizing the complexity of the task, Bawa apprenticed with the local architect H. H. Reid and went on to complete studies in architecture in England between 1953 and 1956. Bawa became a partner in Reid's

In her recent projects, Singh portrays the architecture of Geoffrey Bawa and Studio Mumbai.

Tausif Noor

Singh's images offer a world in which the loftiest aspirations of modernism are realized.

firm in Ceylon in 1957, and throughout the 1960s and 1970s designed private homes, hotels, and schools across the island—renamed Sri Lanka in 1972—and later in Indonesia, Singapore, and Fiji.

Singh recalls her first visit to the Kandalama Hotel—designed by Bawa on the outskirts of Dambulla, in 1994—as a kind of déjà vu experience. Her arrival at the Lunuganga estate in Bentota felt similarly fated. For her *Bawa Series* (2016–ongoing), Singh photographed the interiors of Bawa's estate, as well as a modernist domicile he designed for the artist Ena de Silva in 1960, which was moved brick by brick from Colombo to Lunuganga.

Singh's photographs highlight Bawa's meticulous selection of materials to create contrast, a hallmark of the so-called tropical modernism associated with his legacy. Consider how the rough, jagged surface of an outside portico's tear-shaped stone pillar harmonizes with the whitewashed walls and glass windows, or the way the curves of the molded chairs in Bawa's living room balance its wide floor-to-ceiling windows, shaded by reed screens.

Harmony with the local environment is also central to the practice of Mumbai-based Bijoy Jain, whose studio work was recently the subject of an exhibition at the Fondation Cartier in Paris. Born in 1965, Jain studied architecture in the United States and worked for Richard Meier before founding an eponymous firm in 1995, later renamed Studio Mumbai. For *Studio Mumbai* (2019–ongoing), Singh made a series of images at the former tobacco warehouse in the south Mumbai enclave of Byculla that serves as Jain's studio space. "There is something I am seeking when I am photographing architecture," she says. "It's not the architects, but this exhalation that I find again and again in Studio Mumbai's work." Singh trained her camera on surface textures of concrete and wood to draw out formal homologies within the studio: a large overstuffed spherical form rhymes with a nearby wall hanging, the folds of the fabric creating further associations. In one image, a trio of folding chairs hangs on a wall above a low wooden daybed.

Jain, who acknowledged his respect for Bawa's precision and dogged devotion to local material and craft in his 2012 Geoffrey Bawa Memorial Lecture, illustrates here that a pared-down approach can open up new possibilities. That ethos is not unlike Singh's, whose spare, monochromatic images of domestic space highlight how constraint offers a way to channel creative energies and draw new connections across different forms and media. Metabolizing the elemental principles shared by photography and architecture, and allowing these connections to take center stage, Singh's images offer a world in which the loftiest aspirations of modernism—to create better living conditions through careful design—are realized.

Tausif Noor is a critic and curator whose writing has appeared in *Frieze*, the *New Yorker*, and the *New York Times*.

Pages 69–73:
From *Bawa Series*,
2016–ongoing; pages
74–77: from *Studio
Mumbai*, 2019–ongoing
Courtesy the artist

THE DESIGN ISSUE

Daniel Shea
Empire Plaza

A Utopian
Dream in Albany

Julian Rose

Of all the epithets coined by New York governor Nelson Rockefeller's opponents to describe his monumental redevelopment plan for the seat of state government in Albany—and there were many, ranging from "Nelson's Pyramid" to "Rocky's Edifice Complex" to an array of creative if mostly unprintable plays on the resonance between his notorious penchant for philandering and the primordial symbolism of a nice big tower—the one that must have stung the most was "Brasília North."

This was not just a riff on the governor's pharaonic ambition, or a dig at his Freudian drive to outdo a father who, after putting the family name on Rockefeller Center, had become the most famous developer in the world. It was a statement of fact: the Albany project really was inspired in part by the Brazilian capitol, which Rockefeller had visited and admired. His chosen architect, Wallace Harrison, had worked closely with Brasília's main architect, Oscar Niemeyer, on the United Nations headquarters in Manhattan (itself built on land purchased by Rockefeller in a deal funded by his father). When Harrison's first drawings for the Albany complex were released, in 1962, their debt to Niemeyer was obvious. And by mocking this connection, the

governor's detractors were attacking not only his vanity but one of his core beliefs: a profound faith in the transformative power of modern architecture.

Rockefeller was an evangelist for modernism in all forms. He was a long-time trustee and sometime president of "mother's museum," as he called the Museum of Modern Art in New York, referring to Abby Aldrich Rockefeller, one of its founders. And just as the museum's pioneering programming was devoted to exploring and promoting connections between all fields of modern visual culture, so did Rockefeller believe that he could combine art and architecture to create magnificent public spaces and monuments that would celebrate the modern era. For Albany, he and Harrison envisioned five massive towers, rising like monoliths surrounding an immense elevated plaza, their severity offset by a performing arts center rendered as a supersized Brancusi-esque form (locals would christen it "the Egg"), with the whole complex anchored by a colossal cultural building housing a library and museum.

The governor also made sure to include plenty of human-scaled artworks. Integrated throughout the complex was the Empire State Plaza Art Collection,

Albany, 2023

Shea's images help us look beyond the clichés of architectural history.

which grew to nearly one hundred modernist paintings and sculptures, including works by such marquee names as Helen Frankenthaler and Jackson Pollock. Whether in the mute sleekness of International Style facades or the exuberant brushwork of Action Painting, Rockefeller had a marked preference for abstraction. As he told a journalist inquiring about the Albany collection, "I like strong, simple painting without a message." For a politician, this aversion to messaging made practical sense. An Abstract Expressionist could be trusted not to paint Lenin's face into the seat of a corporate empire, as Diego Rivera had infamously done in a mural in the main lobby of Rockefeller Center. But there was an idealism here too. Rockefeller saw modernist abstraction as a kind of pure beauty, untainted by ideology and un-

compromised by content, that was ideally suited to uplifting the free American spirit. And so he set out to create what he called "the most beautiful state capitol in America," a place for integrating art into the life of the people.

Unfortunately, the people didn't see it that way. Brasília may have originated in a burst of postwar democratic nation-building, but a 1964 military coup in Brazil shifted the optics of its monumentality toward something more sinister. It didn't help that to make room for his Albany complex, Rockefeller followed the playbook of New York's notorious master builder Robert Moses, using eminent domain to clear ninety-eight acres and displacing some seven thousand residents. The city's mayor spoke for many of his constituents when he railed against the development as "what might be expected in a dictatorship." By the time the complex was finally finished, in 1978, the newly christened Governor Nelson A. Rockefeller Empire State Plaza seemed to embody the very worst of modernism: rigid, authoritarian, out of touch, inhuman.

Yet by studiously avoiding the clichés of architectural photography, Daniel Shea's images of Empire State Plaza help us look beyond the clichés of architectural history that have accumulated around these buildings. It is tempting to assume that architecture's concreteness—its material specificity, its definition of space—translates into a singularity of meaning, as if a building embodies just one thing. But the photographs show that buildings embody nothing so much as contradiction. Shea captures the startling disjunction between Harrison's buildings and their context, but he also catches more mundane and plebeian moments—surfaces, details, and textures familiar in their banality.

When we look past our smug assumptions about an outmoded modernist idiom, we see that it may never have been the heart of the project. "I don't have time to worry about style," Harrison told a reporter in 1966, before pointing out that he had already seen one billion dollars' worth of real estate constructed from his designs. The Albany project would eventually cost two billion, tripling the value of his portfolio. Rockefeller raised that capital by inventing a new way to sell public bonds without voter approval, a strategy born from the advice of a cabal of financial wizards that included his brother David, CEO of Chase Manhattan—"if you think the architecture is imaginative,

consider the financing of the project," quipped a financial analyst for *Newsday*. The buildings don't symbolize authoritarian power as much as ingeniously leveraged debt—not the end of modern architecture but the beginning of the financialization of urban space.

If this is all beginning to sound familiar, try squinting at another giant platform, utterly disdainful of its surroundings and sprouting enormous towers into the sky, that was recently constructed some 150 miles south. Behind the increased density and more up-to-date architectural style, the parallels between New York's Hudson Yards and Albany's Empire State Plaza are almost uncanny. Besides the alienating scale and vast, empty plaza, there's even a cartoonishly grandiose architectural sculpture—the Egg has become the Vessel—and an onsite cultural institution known as the Shed. But there was no need for Hudson Yards' developers to circumvent voters' wishes, because in today's later-stage oligarchy, the government's role in development is to rewrite laws—usually some combination of rezoning and tax incentives—to ensure maximum profits and then get out of the way.

We can draw a line from Albany to the far West Side, but things could have turned out differently. Rockefeller dwarfed his spending on the capitol complex with the State University Construction Fund, which eventually spent four billion dollars on thirty new campuses and increased enrollment in the SUNY system under his leadership from fewer than forty thousand students to more than a quarter of a million. In retrospect, the most anachronistic thing about the Empire State Plaza isn't the modernist architecture; it's the commitment, however misguided, to the public good.

Julian Rose is a historian and critic of art and architecture based in New York.

This page:
Albany, 2023

Opposite, foreground:
Brasília Palace III, 2018;
background: Albany, 2023

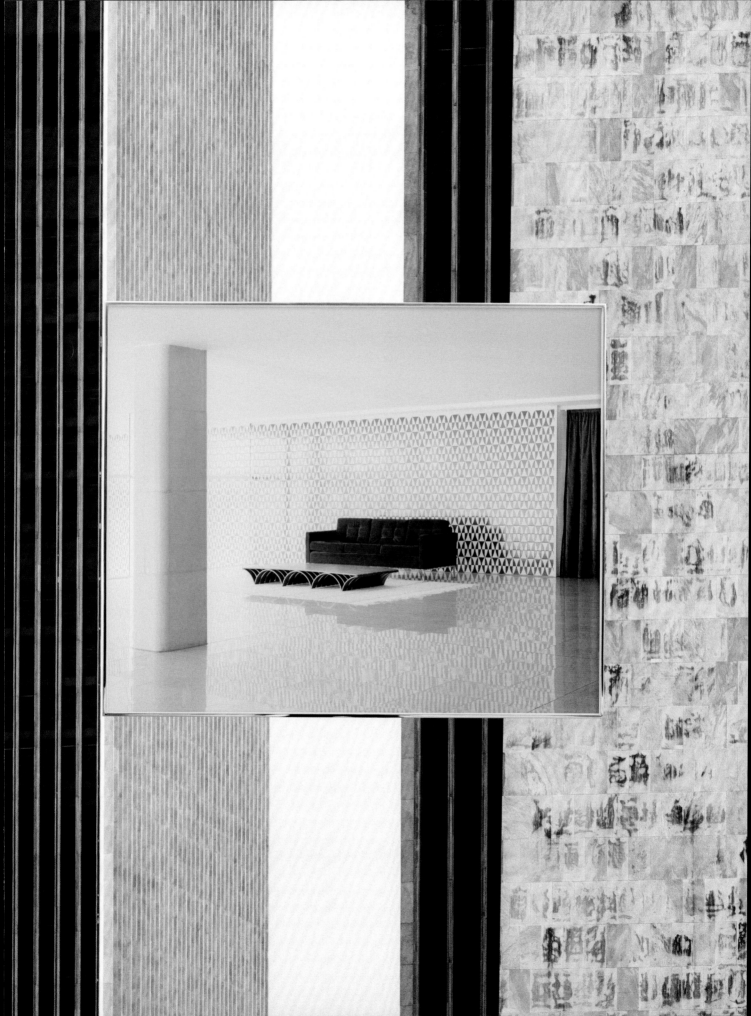

This page:
Albany, 2023

Opposite:
New York City
Construction, 2017

Alice Rawsthorn Design Touches Everything

The design writer and critic Alice Rawsthorn counts the photographer and filmmaker László Moholy-Nagy as one of her heroes. Her book of essays *Design as an Attitude* draws its title from Moholy-Nagy's *Vision in Motion*, in which he argued for the connections between art and life, and how design is characterized by resourcefulness, invention, and the needs of a community.

This principle carries through Rawsthorn's work, where she consistently champions design's potential to address complex challenges facing societies around the globe. In 2020, Rawsthorn cofounded the Design Emergency project with the Museum of Modern Art curator Paola Antonelli, to investigate the design response to the COVID-19 pandemic. The project started with an Instagram account. It's now also a podcast, YouTube channel, and a book, *Design Emergency: Building a Better Future*. The initiative swiftly expanded to tell stories of how designers are reacting to ecological and sociopolitical emergencies, and how advances in communication and technology are influencing change. These are themes that Rawsthorn has previously investigated in her design columns for the *New York Times*. Last winter, writer Billie Muraben met Rawsthorn at her London home, where they spoke about how stories of design are often told through photographs.

Billie Muraben: **With Design Emergency, why was it important for you and Paola Antonelli to have an open definition, or interpretation, of what design is and who designers are?**

Alice Rawsthorn: Well, I can't think of any other way of defining design. And Design Emergency really reflects the vision of design that I've shared as a writer, and that Paola has shared in her exhibitions. The books *Hello World: Where Design Meets Life* (2013) and *Design as an Attitude* (2018) were predicated on the notion that affordable, easily accessible, incredibly powerful digital technology was transforming, or had transformed, the practice and possibilities of design. It liberated designers from the restricted roles they played during the industrial age, when design was routinely stereotyped as a styling and promotional tool, generally under the instruction of someone else. Designers have been liberated to work independently and to pursue their own social, political, and ecological goals. We developed the idea for Design Emergency initially as a response to the COVID-19 crisis, at the start of the first lockdown.

BM: **Design Emergency features the research and practice of highly skilled designers and many brilliant examples of improvisation by people working in the moment with available resources and being responsive to their immediate context, whether that is the COVID-19 pandemic, natural disasters, or sociopolitical turmoil.**

AR: We began by identifying what we saw as the key areas of all our lives, in the broadest possible sense, that needed positive design interventions. We then identified the people who, we believe, were at the forefront of innovation in those fields and who, crucially, had already delivered practical projects. While they might also engage in a lot of purely experimental or conceptual work, they had to have proven that their approach would work, because we wanted to reach a general audience beyond the committed design community.

We drew a list of all the complex challenges we face, but also the opportunities, and then identified who was tackling them. One of the joys of design, particularly if you write about it, is (a) it's a ubiquitous force in our lives, so it touches absolutely everything, and (b) it

Page 88:
Alice Rawsthorn at Donlon Books, London, February 2024
Photograph by Daragh Soden for *Aperture*

We began by identifying what we saw as the key areas of all our lives that needed positive design interventions.

can be interpreted in so many different ways by different people. Some of the people we interviewed work in what could be seen as a more conventional form of design, but they have all done so in a really exemplary, innovative, original, and iconoclastic way. A wonderful example is Irma Boom, the book designer. Book design is one of the oldest conventional areas of design, with centuries of rich and inspiring history. And Irma is so brilliant, she has reinvented it completely.

BM: **How does photography come into Design Emergency as a research tool, or otherwise?**

AR: All sorts of new photographic technologies have been made available, many of which have enriched and empowered design. Also, many of them are particularly pertinent to terrible emergencies of different types. If you think of the climate emergency and photography's impact on that in terms of design, until recently photography—other than in photojournalism—played a relatively restricted role. But that has changed dramatically, partly because the technological changes of satellite images, drones, and advances in geospatial imagery have completely transformed the way we can visualize the climate emergency.

One strategic design project I'm interested in is the Great Green Wall in Africa, which is the epic design endeavor to cultivate vegetation across a five-thousand-mile strip of the southern edge of the Sahara Desert, from Senegal to Djibouti. That is very difficult to portray at scale, but the satellite imagery, particularly from the ESA [European Space Agency], has done so brilliantly.

BM: **And what about individual photographers?**

AR: One example would be the Bangladeshi photographer Asif Salman, who works with Marina Tabassum, the humanitarian architect. Bangladesh is a country at the forefront of reinventing the design of flood defenses by moving away from the gray infrastructure of concrete dams, which we know doesn't work, to literally letting flooding flow naturally to irrigate the land and, ultimately, cause far less damage. His photography of Marina's work has not only made people realize how effective that has been, but he humanizes all her projects.

Similarly, Iwan Baan—who is a famous architectural photographer and has produced very intelligent and elegant images of works by architects including Rem Koolhaas, Herzog & de Meuron, and so on—recently did a body of photographs for the Room for the River project in the Netherlands, which, again, is all about the switch from gray infrastructure to naturalistic flood defenses.

BM: **How can photography contribute to investigative design research and respond to issues such as refugee crises?**

AR: There's been incredible photojournalism in that field, with large-scale satellite images showing the sheer scale of refugee settlements like the Za'atari camp in Jordan and the Cox's Bazar settlements in Bangladesh, which, I think, have more than a million people living there. But also the work of photographers such as Salman, who's humanized the crisis, and the Italian photographer Matteo de Mayda, who for years has traveled to refugee settlements but has also done a lot of photography of the support for migrants in Italy.

If you look at investigative design research, which is a hugely important, rapidly expanding new area of design, photography is absolutely integral. Groups like Formafantasma, the Italian design studio run by Andrea Trimarchi and Simone Farresin, have mounted long-term investigations of complex and contentious areas of our lives that have seldom been explored, such as the gigantic, often illicit global trade in digital waste and the ecological damage caused by the international timber industry.

BM: **Forensic Architecture, the multi-disciplinary research group that investigates state violence and human rights violations, makes use of photography to reconstruct crime scenes, sites of conflict, and other architectural spaces to communicate evidence.**

AR: Forensic Architecture has been one of the great design phenomena of recent years, and one of the first people I wanted to interview for Design Emergency was its founder Eyal Weizman. He's absolutely extraordinary. He says that it's all down to not just smartphones but the first feeble cell phones that could make photographs with just a few kilobytes, which basically empowered citizens to witness instances of abuse and criminality, and to provide evidence that could be used for government policy reviews and legal cases to secure justice for victims.

And it's not just photography that has contributed to this, it's the whole phenomenon of open-source intelligence, everything from CCTV-footage apps such as Find My, satellite imagery, and video clips. All of this is analyzed by Forensic Architecture and the teams of relevant specialists that it assembles to investigate climate crimes, miscarriages of justice, contested killings, and so on.

BM: **Open-source intelligence is being used and analyzed more widely, as a way to prove or contest claims during conflict.**

AR: At the *New York Times*, or even BBC Verify, where journalists analyze and visualize evidence, there are less complex and sophisticated investigations than Forensic Architecture's, but there are important ones, particularly at a time of such horrific catastrophes and emergencies as those we have now. You see the impact that open-source intelligence has had on Russia's war against Ukraine. The number of claims and counterclaims that the Ukrainians were able to verify because they did have CCTV footage of

Installation view of
Formafantasma and
Joanna Piotrowska,
Sub Rosa, ARCH Athens,
2020. Photograph by
Paris Tavitian
Courtesy the artists

One of the things I love about Tillmans's work is the way that he investigates the materiality of daily life.

what actually happened, or people had recorded it, or snapped it on their phones, has been very moving. It's been absolutely essential in Gaza, from which international journalists were expelled at a very early part of the conflict, especially as both sides release information that's immediately contested and contradicted by the other.

BM: **Your book *Design as an Attitude* explores design as an agent of social, political, and ecological change. The title comes from László Moholy-Nagy's 1947 book *Vision in Motion*. How has he been important to your thinking?**

AR: I've always found Moholy-Nagy to be this really thrilling, charismatic, dynamic figure, constantly committed to experimentation and intellectual inquiry, very open and generous. And also, his first wife, Lucia Moholy, I find her fascinating too. She was, of course, a highly influential photographer. He was responsible for many great feats, not least the championing of film and new approaches to photography—and also the development of an early cultural critique about them.

He saw them as having a huge influence over cultural change in years to come, and that was something he worked on with Lucia Moholy very closely. He reconceptualized design by identifying a relevant and productive role that liberated it from the constraints of the industrial age.

BM: **Lucia Moholy's photographs from the 1920s have influenced how the Bauhaus school in Dessau has been seen and understood.**

AR: She's a fascinating example of the old-school relationship of design and photography, demonstrating how a photographer who is really passionate about a particular city at a particular time, or a particular movement, or another phenomenon, can produce work that's so powerful and so compelling that it goes on to dominate—not in a negative sense but in a very positive sense, an enlivening sense—public perceptions of that phenomenon. You could also think of people like Julius Shulman on mid-century modernist architecture in the Los Angeles area, and Berenice Abbott on modernism in early twentieth-century New York.

Lucia Moholy cataloged the daily life of the Bauhaus. She also pioneered what became the dominant typology for industrial-design photography for the twentieth century, because Moholy-Nagy really championed the industrialization of product design. They are beautifully composed. They are very fetishized. They are in black and white. There are no shadows. And industrial objects have been photographed in the same fetishistic, generally no-shadows manner ever since.

BM: **The work of the designer Alessandro Mendini and Superstudio from the 1970s are similarly characterized by photography—for example, when Mendini designed the Lassù chair and then set fire to it with a photographer capturing the event. Another example is Superstudio's photo collages of unbuildable buildings and scenes that imagined utopian futures or poked fun at the status quo. The ideas are kept alive through documentation.**

AR: You are absolutely right. Many of Superstudio's projects were wholly unrealized and became increasingly

Wolfgang Tillmans,
Headlight (f), 2012
© the artist and courtesy Regen Projects, Los Angeles

unrealizable and fantastical, which is very appealing but also very sad.

BM: **A completely different but related point is Wolfgang Tillmans's interest in photographing man-made objects and structures. I went to see him interview Rem Koolhaas a few years ago and Tillmans asked him, "You've designed so many buildings, yet still, I'll go to your public buildings and the queue for the women's loos is a mile long, and there's no queue for the men's loos. Why haven't you just started**

This page:
Lucia Moholy, *Liqueur*
Pitcher and Ashtray, **1924**
Courtesy Harvard Art
Museums

Opposite:
Superstudio, *Gli Atti*
Fondamentali,
Educazione, **from**
Educazione 3, **1971-72**
© Cristiano Toraldo di
Francia

**designing your buildings with twice
the number of loos for women?"**

AR: Wow. Full marks to Tillmans for
asking such an incisive question, which
doesn't surprise me at all. There are a
number of artists over the years who
have interrogated design in a particularly
intelligent and imaginative way. Richard
Hamilton would be another example,
and Tillmans is undoubtedly among them.
One of the things I really love about his
work is the way that he investigates the
materiality of daily life.

My favorite of all these projects was
a series of photographs he made of car
headlights, which have been a minor
obsession of mine for a really long time.
Over the last ten years, there's been an
explosion of technological development
in car lighting. As a result, automotive
designers have become ever more theat-
rical, flamboyant, and sophisticated in
their treatment of them. It's a very jugular
interpretation of industrial design that
I've found really interesting—and it
certainly enlivened nighttime drives

around London. So I was thrilled to discover that Tillmans is a fellow obsessive.

BM: **What projects are on your desk
right now?**

AR: I have just started work on a new
book, *Design and Identity,* which, as the
title suggests, will explore the diverse
ways in which we have designed identities of diverse types—personal, political,
institutional, national, local, and so on—
in different geographies at different
times and with different objectives. And
Paola Antonelli and I are preparing for
the fifth year of Design Emergency,
which feels unreal. When we launched
it, neither of us would have dreamt that
it would be thriving after so long.

Billie Muraben is a design writer and
independent curator based in London.
She was the assistant curator of the 5th
Istanbul Design Biennial in 2021.

Off the Wall

Exhibitions have always been arenas for experimentation with design.

David Campany and Sara Knelman

With no inherent relation to scale, materiality, or context, the photographic image is a response to not only its subject but also the myriad possible forms it can take. After image "capture" comes output, and the choices of output are almost unlimited. The image might be printed on the pages of books and magazines, blown up into billboards or murals, incorporated into sculpture, painted over, collaged, projected, illuminated, compressed, digitized, or networked. And none of these formats need be definitive: the image can (and very often does) change shape, adapt, evolve, and exist in different states simultaneously.

For photography, the space of exhibition has frequently been an arena for experimentation and a forum for exploring relations to associated fields such as graphic design, architecture, and networked tools of communication. The image itself is only part of the equation; the form it takes is critical to determining who sees it, how it is experienced, and the ways in which it might be interpreted. The first known displays of photography were small affairs in government offices and institutions in London and Paris, where an elite audience marveled at the newly invented medium. In the 1850s, photography found the public through industrial expositions. The turn of the twentieth century saw a shift from crowded salon-style hangs to the minimalist, single-row convention of the white cube and adventurous modes of display related to the dynamics of advertising, cinema, and magazines.

The page is the first place for most photographs. From the 1920s through the '40s, in particular, the emergence of photographic modernism in cultural centers around the world was indebted to photography journals. The Bauhaus in Germany, Surrealism in France and elsewhere, and the revolutionary tactics of Soviet photography advanced a new spirit of experimentation and social potential. At the same time, sustained interest from public museums brought photography into a different relation to art and art history, raising new questions and ambitions for the medium.

The potential of scale became an urgent consideration as galleries and museums began to occupy postindustrial spaces and accommodate increasingly immersive, experiential installations. Printing technology and the commercial market have led to larger and larger pictures, and in some cases size seems a pure response to market demand. Yet questions of scale have also occasioned some highly considered exhibitions and work that balances a photograph's connections to the human body, to the world of things it represents, and to the function and architecture of the spaces in which it is displayed.

Photography has also increasingly occupied three dimensions, as artists consider photographic ideas through interdisciplinary materials. Outside the prescribed spaces of exhibition, the exchange and transmission of images across media has been a way for photographers to build networks and for institutions to connect to communities. Resisting institutional agendas, biennials and festivals often take images outdoors, co-opting spaces of advertising and public display and encouraging experimentation and innovation.

A few years ago, a show at the Metropolitan Museum of Art considered unfinished artworks. There were no photographs on view, perhaps because photography is always unfinished. The raw image—a negative or a digital file, maybe even a loose print—is only one stage in a photograph's becoming. The next stages determine how it circulates in the world, and in particular how it connects to cultures of display. Photography's relation to the spaces of exhibition is most often informed by design decisions, and it is here that the medium makes its important connections to graphics, scenography, and architecture. What follows is a selection of experimental presentations that embody these ideas.

David Campany is a writer, curator, and photographer based in London.

Sara Knelman is a writer and curator based in Toronto, and the executive director and publisher of C *Magazine*.

William Klein, Paris, 1986–87

William Klein began his career as a painter in the late 1940s, with ambitions to work at mural scale. His move into street photography, fashion, and abstract darkroom work came with the realization that photography has no inherent materiality, dimension, or context. It can be any size, belonging equally to walls, pages, or screens. For many years, Klein concentrated on graphically innovative work for *Vogue* and other magazines, a string of rule-breaking photobooks (focusing on New York, Rome, Moscow, and Tokyo), which he designed himself, and documentary and feature films. In 1986, he returned to exhibitions with *Le commun des mortels*. Its centerpiece was a double-sided, winding ribbon of his signature group street portraits, drawn from all phases of his career and printed up to nine feet wide. As on the page, the images were scaled to the available space, without visible white borders. Klein once said of his photobooks, "Only the sequencing counts . . . as in a movie." In the exhibition, the photographs unfolded like an epic tracking shot.

Installation view of *William Klein: Le commun des mortels*, 1986–87, Centre National de Photographie, Palais de Tokyo, Paris
Courtesy Studio William Klein

Geraldo de Barros, São Paulo, 1951

In the late 1940s, the experiments in abstract photography of the Brazilian artist Geraldo de Barros (1923–1998) coincided with the establishment of the Museu de Arte de São Paulo (MASP), designed by the Italian-born architect Lina Bo Bardi. The creative energies of both artist and architect, each committed to the social potential of modernist forms, merged in de Barros's 1951 exhibition at the museum. A culmination of what he termed his *fotoformas*, the display heightened the geometric industrial themes and patterns of his photograms and montages, which were often created with the material use of industrial objects and mechanisms, such as the insertion of computer punch cards into the lens of the enlarger. Bo Bardi's exhibition design brought the works away from the wall, hanging them instead at varying heights from floor-to-ceiling aluminum poles. Shortly after the exhibition, de Barros would abandon photography, turning instead to engraving, text, and industrial design.

Installation view of *Geraldo de Barros: Fotoformas*, 1951, Museu de Arte São Paulo
Courtesy Instituto Moreira Salles, Rio de Janeiro

Kelly Lycan, Vancouver, 2014

Alfred Stieglitz's Little Galleries of the Photo-Secession—aka 291, the gallery's address on Fifth Avenue in New York—was a pivotal space for photography from 1905 to 1917. Over the years it gained a kind of mythic status, due in part to Stieglitz's international journal *Camera Work*, which chronicled the gallery's activities, including installation images, reproductions of works, and detailed descriptions of its design, such as the diffuse lighting and carefully selected paint hues and textiles. In 2014, the Canadian artist Kelly Lycan set out to create a full-scale replica, not of the gallery itself but of its image. Lycan's architectural installation, devoid of photographs, self-consciously mimics a black-and-white photograph, taken by Stieglitz, of a 1906 exhibition of Pictorialist photography. Depending on the angle of approach, Lycan's constructed image may materialize the rich tones and textures of Stieglitz's original space, or reveal the raw wood propping up the facade. "I was interested," Lycan says, "in how an image can exist without an image being present."

Top:
Installation view of Kelly Lycan,
291, From the Faraway Nearby,
2014, Polygon, Vancouver
Courtesy the artist

Bottom:
Installation view of *Gertrude
Käsebier and Clarence H. White*,
1906, 291, New York
Wikimedia Commons

Sophie Ristelhueber, Arles, 2006

In 2006, Sophie Ristelhueber visited the London office of the Reuters news agency to review hundreds of hours of video footage of bomb craters produced during the Iraq War. She made screenshots and later combined these with her own images of similar situations in Turkmenistan, Syria, and the West Bank. These composites looked both real and imaginary, with odd changes in scale and spatial dislocation, not quite specific and not quite universal. During the French photography festival Les Rencontres d'Arles, they were installed as wallpaper prints in the recently vacated luxury apartment of the governor of the Banque de France. The empty rooms provided a jarring context for the empty craters of another world, although on a more abstract, geopolitical level, they were part of the same world order. The series title, *Eleven Blowups*, refers to both the enlargement of the images and the effects of bombs.

Installation view of Sophie Ristelhueber, *Eleven Blowups*, 2006, Les Rencontres d'Arles, France
Courtesy the artist

Installation view of Peter Puklus, *Handbook to the Stars*, 2013, International Festival of Fashion, Photography and Fashion Accessories, Hyères, France
Courtesy the artist

Peter Puklus, Hyères, 2012

Handbook to the Stars (2012) was the first publication by Peter Puklus. With images in different registers—from photographs of sculptural constructions to domestic still life arrangements—it proposes a constellation rather than a sequence, allowing for open connections in different directions. The images do not sit squarely on the book's spreads but seem to flow over their edges, the remaining parts appearing on adjacent pages. Held in the hand, the content is viewed just one spread at a time, and the connections remain tentative. In exhibition, however, thirty copies of the book can be combined and overlaid, allowing the images to come together. In this way, the experience of *Handbook to the Stars* is unusually specific to its mode of presentation. Where the book is a tactile, personal object, on the wall it becomes a "piece," a sculpture.

Robbie Vaughan & Williams Architects, Expo 67, Montreal

The year 1967 marked Canada's centennial and brought Expo 67, a wildly successful World's Fair, to Montreal. Up to half a million visitors a day would have encountered *The People Tree*, a sixty-six-foot-high, sixty-five-foot-wide maple-tree-shaped structure. Large photographs toned in red, orange, and gold were silk-screened onto nylon "leaves" that swayed in the breeze. A staircase "trunk" allowed visitors to wander among them. The idea, executed by the Still Photography Division of the National Film Board of Canada, was to celebrate the lives of everyday Canadians by showcasing hundreds of portraits captured by photographers across the country. Recalling the landmark 1955 Museum of Modern Art exhibition *The Family of Man*, the government commission sought to emphasize universal human connection and middle-class family life; in retrospect, it also makes obvious the exclusions inherent in such a partial view of the Canadian experience.

**Installation view of Robbie Vaughan & Williams Architects,
The People Tree, 1967, Expo 67, Montreal**
Courtesy RIBA Collections

The
Shape
of
Things

From tombstones to handbags, photographs have long been used to sell just about everything. How do artists make the objects we desire seem irresistible?

Jesse Dorris

IMAGINE HAVING LOST A LOVED one in the New England of the 1870s. Then, a knock at your door: a salesman in a suit. He pulls out a bound catalog of albumen-silver prints, with as many photographs in it as you've maybe seen in a lifetime, each showing a tombstone ready to memorialize your loss. The trade catalog for the Vermont Marble Companies offers a purchase for your grief, documentation that something exists in the here and now to honor those in the here-after. This is an example of what the Metropolitan Museum of Art's research assistant Virginia McBride calls "the truth claim of photography," a way companies used the supposed veracity of photographic images to convince customers they would deliver what they promised.

It's an early highlight of a Met show on view this summer that McBride has curated, *The Real Thing: Unpacking Product Photography*, which tracks how pictures made people familiar with objects for consumption and then, with the arrival of modernism, rendered such objects radiantly unfamiliar. The show, which features work from the nineteenth century to the late 1940s, arrives at a moment when many artists have been drawing inspiration from the long history of how

This page:
Ralph Bartholomew Jr.,
Soap Packaging, 1936;
opposite: Photographer
unknown, *Trade Catalogue
for Producers' Marble and
Vermont Marble Companies*
(detail), 1870s–80s
Courtesy the Metropolitan
Museum of Art, New York

Modernism, with its emerging formal concerns of experimentation and abstraction, was a tool kit for a sales pitch.

photography has been used to sell all manner of commodities. It's a moment marked by a turn from the object for sale to the meaning of the sale itself.

But first you had to make the sale, and the best way to do that was to catch someone's eye. A commercial photographer in Providence, Rhode Island, named H. Raymond Ball photographed a comb from an unknown manufacturer balancing mysteriously on its edge; in his *Pocket Comb* (ca. 1930s), the expanse of the object's shadow somehow echoes both the architect Eero Saarinen's Gateway Arch in St. Louis and the bob hairstyle favored by flappers. "It's an object lesson in what the camera can do with the right light and the right shadow and any object at all," McBride explained.

Corporate resources funded adventurous photographers to push things even further. Edward J. Steichen was commissioned by a Swiss textile manufacturer to lend their products a touch of the new. His *"Sugar Lumps" Pattern Design for Stehli Silks*, from the 1920s, staggers rows of the treat to cleverly arrange their shadows into a fresh take on a checkerboard; in 1927, Stehli made a textile with Steichen's photograph printed upon it, and the advertisement itself became the product.

August Sander went even further. For *Osram Light Bulbs* (ca. 1930) he composed a spiral of lightbulbs, creating a gelatin-silver print that seems lit vertiginously from within. If the bulbs could do that on a magazine page, what wonders they might lend to your house! In such advertisements, photography transcends its lifelike authority to become life itself, abuzz with a kind of optimism some Americans in the 1930s and '40s might've found lacking in their daily lives, as they flicked through Depression-era fashion magazines and war-stricken newspapers.

Ralph Bartholomew Jr.'s carbo print *Soap Packaging* (1936) erects a cityscape of candy-colored packaged soap on newsprint in a bubbly anticipation of Piet Mondrian's *Broadway Boogie Woogie* six years later. An unknown image maker gassed up a car ad with the latest editing techniques for *Montage for Packard Super Eight* (ca. 1940), which you can imagine zipping around that soap package city, even if that many people couldn't possibly fit in a Packard that size. Modernism, with its emerging formal concerns of experimentation and abstraction, was an irresistible tool kit for a sales pitch.

This fizzy blend of commercial seduction and fine-art methodology reached a peak in the pages of *Vogue*, which commissioned Irving Penn's *Theatre Accident, New York* (1947). "It's not usually talked about as a product photograph, but rather sort of the be-all and end-all of photographic still lifes of the twentieth century," McBride said. And yet, every object spilled from that purse is available for purchase—and *has* been purchased by the sophisticated kind of woman *Vogue* suggests you should be. "The idea that these amalgamated objects can really create an entire personhood is very explicitly spelled out," she added. "Even with these inanimate objects, [Penn] could conjure a living, breathing woman." In the eighty or so years between the tombstone catalog and the *Vogue* masterpiece, photography moved from the lifelike, to larger-than-life, to having the ability to conjure up life itself.

And what happened in the many decades after the photographers shown in *The Real Thing*? Contemporary image makers—who are outside the focus of the museum's presentation and the heirs to its heroes—grew up in thrall of the earlier history it explores. They now live and work in a world of hyperconsumerism, advertising, and targeted marketing that those photographs, and the related capitalist machinery, helped to build. The exhibition's checklist offers a prompt to consider how they made sense of the tug and pull of art and commerce within a picture frame or, increasingly, the social-media grid.

"Sometimes it feels like all I'm really looking at is this strange reflection of what happens when a person is fed advertising their entire life and, weirdly, fetishizes it," the photographer Bobby Doherty told me. His images—from eye-popping sweets and consumer goods of clients including Balenciaga and Apple to the still lifes filling his recent photobook, *Dream About Nothing* (2023)—draw on the legacy established by giants such as Penn but bring a sense of irony and intentional awkwardness. Doherty's color palette is often hyperreal and exaggerated, but it can be muted to recall another era. "I just sometimes feel like there isn't a new way to do it," he said with a sigh. "The rules were really clearly laid out, and deviating from them just takes it to a place that isn't advertising anymore." His image *Oronamin C* (2022) features soda bottles and what appears to be a

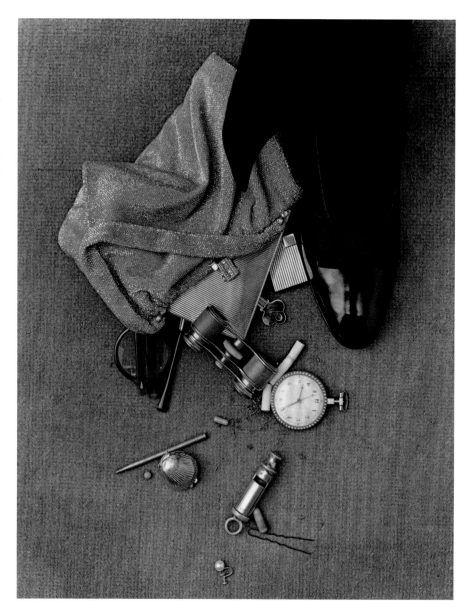

Irving Penn, *Theatre Accident, New York*, 1947
Courtesy the Irving Penn Foundation and the Metropolitan Museum of Art, New York

cheeseburger on a mirrored surface, and was inspired by 1960s food advertisements. The goal of his book, he added, was to create an experience of "subliminal advertising in a dream."

For the conceptual artist Christopher Williams, histories of technology, production, and modernization are told through almost absurdist pile-ups of information, with captions elongated into campuses of text. His images re-create the aesthetics of a product photograph and the mechanics of image making, but often nod to political and colonial histories. His recent image of an IKEA kitchen treats a mass-produced interior model with a cartographical rigor you sense he might not quite think it deserves. Who would want to live in a world like this, with its banal perfection, the photograph seems to ask, while at the same time

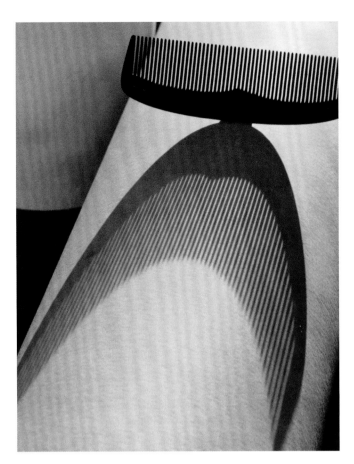

marshaling every resource of advertising. It's less a swoon than a wink. Williams's occasional photographs of models, seen in his work referencing a Kodak reflection guide from the 1960s, present them smiling broadly—a real no-no in the images used by fashion e-commerce sites, such as SSENSE, that feature both product and editorial. How could anyone in this world possibly be this happy?

The impact, emotional or otherwise, of accumulation seems to fuel Sara Cwynar's work as she plumbs e-commerce spaces for evidence of what, or maybe *how*, companies think people want now. Which might just be *more*: yesterday's brand catalog is today's social-media feed, with endless scrolls of SSENSE or Shein items presented by similar models in similar poses. These posts could be purses spilling out glamorous contents, but there's little personality on display.

Cwynar's series *Marilyn* (2020) included photographs she took of SSENSE models in the company's signature trio of poses, re-created on larger scales and with harsher lighting, as if trying to blow out the halo effect. "You can't figure out what's real, or what something actually looks like, or whether you're looking at the same person or just the same image

with different outfits photoshopped on," she said. "I like the confusion of different styles of commercial photography in one thing. That kind of digital plenitude, there being too much to contend with, so everything starts to feel kind of value-less." And yet value is in the eye of the beholder: Dior invited Cwynar to collaborate on a handbag.

In the 1990s, such a collaboration might have been decried as "selling out." At that moment—when international corporations were consolidating media into the hands of a very few, and the techniques of modernism had become all-too-familiar, even sinister—artists' efforts to resist the collapse between art and product often felt noble. Even if, as the Met show makes clear, photographers were always working across contexts. Roe Ethridge came up in the '90s moment when selling out might be taboo; today, with fewer markets for photography, he thinks that notion is passé. Instead, he trades on the notion of value, working for high-end fashion brands and showing the same images in high-end galleries. Confusion might be the point—or, perhaps, a tactic to wrangle with the challenges he sees in commercial photography. "How do I depict a handbag in

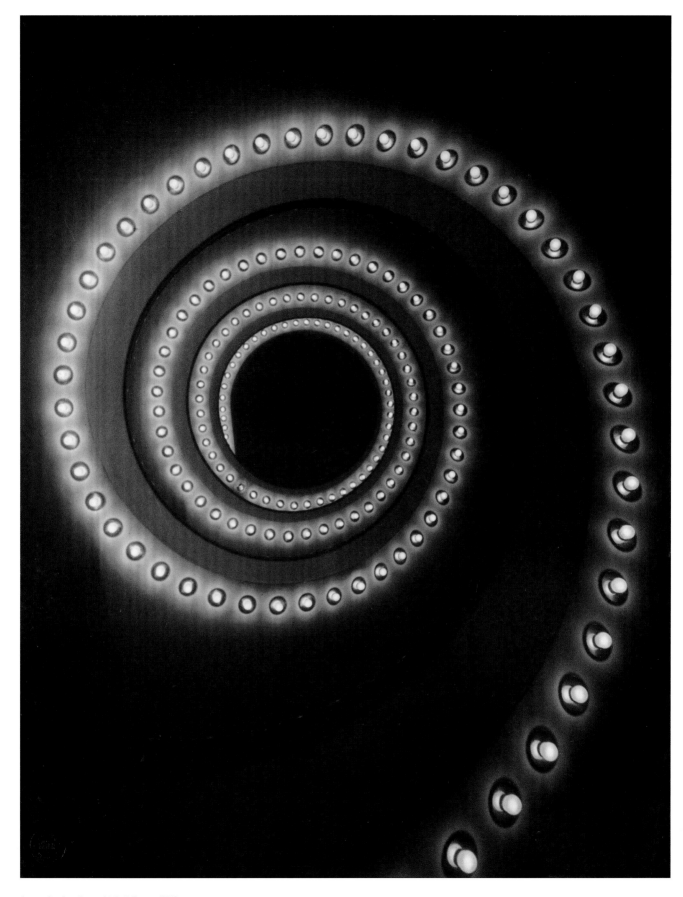

August Sander, *Osram Light Bulbs,* **ca. 1930**
Courtesy the Metropolitan Museum of Art,
New York

This page, top:
Christopher Williams,
*Blocking Template:
IKEA Kitchen
(Overhead Nr. 2)
Studio Thomas Borho,
Oberkasseler Str. 39,
Düsseldorf, Germany
September 7, 2022*, 2023
© the artist and courtesy
David Zwirner, New York

This page, bottom:
Sara Cwynar, *Ali from
SSENSE.com (How to
Marry a Millionaire)*,
from the series *Marilyn*,
2020
Courtesy the artist and
the Approach, London

Opposite:
Bobby Doherty, *Oronamin
C*, 2022, from *Dream
About Nothing*, 2023
Courtesy Loose Joints

a way that's not untruthful to me?" he asked. "Which is a weird thing to think about. Why *would* I like or not like a handbag?" As Penn's handbag does, Ethridge hopes his work "could live without the caption."

These days, images live without all kinds of context, unmoored from their origins and floating freely across our screens. The photographers who made the images in *The Real Thing* proved you could sell anything; today's artists work in a world where you have to sell everything. In the end, we're left with the same question as that salesman at the door: What makes you pay attention? Product photography works—today, when we see too much, it lingers in our minds—because it tells us something about ourselves. It's not about the product itself but what the picture produces inside you. It's not a proof, but a mirror.

**Jesse Dorris is a writer based
in New York and a contributor
to *Aperture*, *Surface*, and the
New Yorker.**

How to Marry a Millionaire, 20th Century, 1953

Coreen Simpson

In the 1980s, Simpson made portraits of New York's artistic and nightlife scenes—and later found success as a jewelry designer. Her multifaceted work tells a singular story.

Thessaly La Force

Past Lives

IN 1983, THE PHOTOGRAPHER and jewelry designer Coreen Simpson began going once a week to the Roxy, a beating heart of New York City's downtown nightlife, where, on select nights, hip-hop music fresh from the Bronx pulsed and throbbed. Simpson, then a forty-one-year-old working mother, was far from a regular. She had recently taken a picture of two young men in fedoras who had caught her eye on the subway, and her daughter had suggested she visit the Roxy, thinking she might find it fertile ground for her portraiture work.

Inside the club, Simpson set up a small makeshift studio. Her boyfriend at the time, the artist George Mingo, came along to watch her equipment while Simpson scouted the dance floor for subjects. On and off, over several years, she photographed whoever caught her eye. Young and fierce, these "kids," as Simpson called them, were always impeccably dressed, sometimes in fedoras and suits adorned with chains, or in fur caps and large hoop earrings.

Rendered in black and white, they look out of time, like gods and goddesses from antiquity, their faces serious and unsmiling, the glory of their youth and beauty undeniable. "I didn't want to make anything trendy, I wanted to capture their style like a *Vogue* photographer. I wanted it to be serious and classic," she told me. Simpson published a selection in *EnFoco*

magazine, a publication devoted to photography, a few years later under the series title *B-Boys*. Over the following decades, her *B-Boys* photographs appeared in various magazines and newspapers as well as in several exhibitions.

Simpson stated that she wanted to give the teenagers from her *B-Boys* series dignity. "I had heard so many negative comments about how they'd never get jobs because they tied their sneakers a certain way," she said in a 1987 interview in *Black American Literature Forum*. "To be a black man in this country must be so difficult. I am a woman, and I know what I have to go against. . . . These kids are locked into a community. They have to deal with the white world which is putting them down all the time." She could be speaking today.

On a recent winter afternoon, I visited Simpson at her home in Crown Heights, Brooklyn. Simpson is tall and charismatic, with a vivacious demeanor. In a leopard-print robe and orange ballet flats, she gave me a quick tour of her apartment, introducing me to her boyfriend of over a decade, Keith Bennett. Simpson had been caring for Bennett full-time since he was diagnosed with cancer.

Born in 1942, Simpson was the elder child of a white private-school teacher and a Black jazz musician. Early on, her mother left Simpson and her brother with their father. Soon after,

Page 110:
Alva with clock,
1991/2021

This page:
George Mingo, Coreen
Simpson wearing her
"Power" necklace with a
view camera, ca. 1970s

Opposite:
Man with curl, ca. 1990s,
from the series *B-Boys*

Young and fierce, these "kids," as Simpson called them, were always impeccably dressed.

they were taken into child protective services. Simpson has memories of her father visiting her and her brother at the orphanage where they were placed. "I remember how sad he was—so sad that that had happened," she said. He later died in a motorcycle accident. The loss profoundly shaped her. "I have no photographs of my biological parents, which might be why I'm drawn to photography, because photographs are so important," Simpson said. "I have no photographs of myself until I'm age six or seven."

When she was six, she and her brother moved to Crown Heights, where they were raised by a working-class Black family. She remembers watching the neighborhood parade while her mother combed her hair on their stoop. "I used to see these fabulous Black people walking down the street with the most amazing outfits," she said. "Because Black people, we do have style. You've got to give it to us. Men wearing orange suits and green suits. They were so handsome, so self-possessed. They had a swagger." Before she knew what a camera was, she fundamentally understood the value of an image. "I used to say in my mind, *Click, click*," she told me. "I was always taking pictures in my head."

It would take several decades, though, before Simpson would pick up a camera professionally. She graduated from Samuel J. Tilden High School in Brooklyn but chose to wait several years before enrolling at the Fashion Institute of Technology (FIT) to learn patternmaking, hoping to be a fashion designer. By day, Simpson worked as a corporate executive secretary. At the time, she was married, with two small children. But she found the technical components of the course challenging and dropped out. And she left her abusive husband, vowing never to remarry.

As a single mother, she began to think again about having a second career, one that was more intellectually and creatively sustaining. She had dabbled in modeling after FIT but decided she didn't want work to be dependent on her looks. Simpson set her sights on journalism instead. She queried *Essence* magazine, asking to contribute a story about traveling for work as a Black woman in Iran. Her day job, as an assistant to the president of an Iranian company based in New York, allowed her to travel to Tehran before the revolution in 1979. "It was fabulous. I met Arab royalty, yes darling, they were so fabulous," she recalled. The story was never published, but it motivated Simpson to keep pitching. With some persistence, she became a contributor to and then an editor at the small independent magazine *Unique New York*, a lifestyle publication about and for Black New Yorkers. Frustrated with the way her stories—profiles of working people, from bartenders to musicians—were being photographed, Simpson began to bring her own camera on assignments, taking portraits of her subjects herself: "I realized, I gotta take pictures myself because no one is going to read my article if the pictures are horrible!"

Though largely an autodidact, she learned how to develop film through a Black street photographer and chemist named Walter Johnson, who operated a darkroom in the Bronx. She also enrolled in a photography class with the artist Frank Stewart at the Studio Museum in Harlem. By the 1980s, Simpson was contributing to a number of publications as both a writer and a photographer, including the *Village Voice*, *Essence*, *Black American*, and *New York Amsterdam News*. The result of that time is an impressive body of work, made both on and off assignment, including portraits of the artist David Hammons,

the actor Eartha Kitt, the singer Diana Ross, the musician Sun Ra, and many others. In a 2022 *New York Times* article about the gallery Just Above Midtown (JAM), New York's first Black-owned art space, founded by Linda Goode Bryant, Simpson is featured alongside Dawoud Bey, Lorraine O'Grady, Randy Williams, and Senga Nengudi. "She was one of the only chroniclers of David Hammons's performances," the curator T. Lax, who organized an exhibition about JAM that opened in fall 2022 at the Museum of Modern Art in New York, said. "We know about these important moments in history through her eye. Coreen, in many ways, was a collaborator or co-participant in much of the work that she was also documenting as a photojournalist."

As a Black woman photographer, Simpson was often on her own. She didn't conform to the stylistic rules of the male-dominated Kamoinge Workshop, a collective of Black photographers established in New York in 1963. And Simpson is older than most of the pioneering Black women photographers who later transformed the art world, such as Carrie Mae Weems and Lorna Simpson. Even as a jobbing photographer, she was isolated. When the *New York Amsterdam News* began sending her to Paris to document the fashion collections each season, she found it impossible to secure a spot in the photographers' pit until Bill Cunningham, the legendary *New York Times* fashion photographer, intervened. "He reached out and took my hand and pulled me to the inner circle," Simpson said. Beautiful portraits of Simpson there—standing in front of the Eiffel Tower, for example—exist, taken by Mingo, who often traveled with her.

"She's long explored the idea of what it means to turn the camera on the self," the artist, photographer, and historian Deborah Willis told me. "It's not only political, it's about beauty. Her self-portraits create a narrative about the self. They're about Black identity. She's found a space to coexist, to be a conceptual artist as well as a photojournalist. In my mind, her work reveals many diverse stories about Black life."

If Black life was her métier as a photographer, her influences were wide-ranging. Some of Simpson's favorite photographers include Diane Arbus, Irving Penn, and Richard Avedon. She admires Weegee for his boldness and flair. She is partial to the delicate lighting in the work of Baron Adolph de Meyer. Beginning in the early 1990s, she started to be more experimental, producing otherworldly collages from the outtakes of her *B-Boys* series, overlaying the back of a head with magazine cutouts such as a timepiece, geometric shapes, or eyes in the hopes of getting creative work. In many of the portraits taken at her then apartment on the Upper West Side, which doubled as her studio, she conjured de Meyer's ethereal and mannered worlds. In one, a friend, the art historian Gylbert Coker, has half her face painted, her throat enclosed with a pearl choker, and wears one of Simpson's hats embellished with tulle blooming into the air. Surreal and contained, they conjure photography from the 1930s, such as Man Ray's images or Carl Van Vechten's portraits of famous writers and artists of the Harlem Renaissance.

Simpson is equally well known for her jewelry designs due to a piece she created in 1990 that became a best-selling phenomenon: the Black Cameo. When Karl Lagerfeld debuted a Coco Chanel cameo in the 1980s, a jewelry client of Simpson's who was an editor at *Essence* suggested Simpson find her a Black cameo, where the silhouette would be the profile of a

This page:
Iman wearing earrings designed by Simpson, ca. 1980s

Opposite:
George Mingo, Simpson wearing her "Pyramid" necklace, Paris, 1986

Black woman instead of a white one. None, however, could be sourced, despite the existence of blackamoor cameos depicting African royalty, which can be dated back to the nineteenth century. Ever the pioneer, Simpson decided to make one herself and found a manufacturer in Rhode Island to execute her vision. In 1994, she licensed the cameo with Avon, and she has been producing variations of them ever since. Simpson's Black Cameo has been worn by celebrities such as Diahann Carroll, Debbie Allen, Kathleen Battle, and Rihanna. "It's both a beautiful object that clearly is an homage to nineteenth century modes of Black women but also just so contemporary," said Lax, who recallled spotting one worn by Studio Museum director Thelma Golden in his archival research of the 1993 Whitney Biennial.

Simpson had been making jewelry for several years before that, selling her designs on the street downtown before moving uptown, across from Bendel's, where wealthy white women liked to shop. "Not Black women, white women with money," she said. "Honey, when I was on 57th Street, the mink coats would be sweeping the ground. They'd be fighting over my things." After she was approached by the fashion designer Carolina Herrera, who bought a dozen necklaces from Simpson for one of her collections, Simpson's pieces began to attract more attention. *Vogue* called her designs "power necklaces." The Cuban singer Celia Cruz became a longtime client and wore Simpson's jewelry on one of her album covers. The supermodel Iman wore Simpson's jewelry on the cover of *Essence*. Simpson moved into a studio on 37th Street and took metalsmithing classes to refine her technique, studying with the jeweler Deborah Aguado at the New School and broadening her offerings to include rings, earrings, and bracelets. Sales were so healthy she was able to stop doing gig photography work to pay the bills.

Lately, in addition to her jewelry business, Simpson is tending to the business of her archive, which she would like to place with a museum or library. Her legacy is important to her. She wants to publish a monograph. But caring for Keith, she admitted, had become time-consuming. A few days after we spoke, Simpson wrote to me saying that Keith had died. She said she was finding solace in distracting herself with work. She doesn't photograph as much as she used to, but she still sees herself as very much a photographer; she showed me her many cameras, some of which were prettily decorated with plastic jewels and glitter. The variety of Simpson's professional interests and accomplishments underscores her talents and passions, along with illustrating how independence and financial security were as important to her as creative freedom.

Thessaly La Force is a writer based in New York.

THE DESIGN ISSUE

Nhu Xuan Hua

Larissa Pham

Dream Sequence

Nhu Xuan Hua's photographs defy easy interpretation. A woman sings karaoke in a shining, armored gown. An archival wedding photograph is beguilingly redacted, dress and suit visible but the bodies of husband and wife absent contours. A black dog gazes out the entrance of a temple—who, or what, is it guarding? Even the simplest image is limned with story; we sense it the way we remember our dreams upon waking. Hua's powerful narrative vision shines through in the clarity of her photographs, which unfold like time passing in slow motion.

Born in Paris to Vietnamese immigrant parents, Hua grew up within a French culture that prized assimilation as a mode of survival. It wasn't until after finishing her studies in photography at the Lycée Auguste Renoir Paris in 2011 and moving to London that Hua was confronted with the question of her origins. "Not enough answers were given by my family," she tells me. "Because when you start asking questions, they say, 'Why, why are you asking, the past belongs to the past.'" In 2016, Hua traveled to Vietnam, beginning an ongoing process of reconnection that has shaped her body of work.

These personal interests seamlessly flow into Hua's commissioned photography. Though she's shot for clients as diverse as Maison Margiela, *Time*, and *British Vogue*, when asked about balancing expectations from brands and publications with her own perspective, she declares: "I take them on board with my vision, along the way with me." Hua's aesthetic propels every assignment, her exhaustive preparation and detailed mood boards merging art and design in the process. For Hua, an editorial campaign can function in two ways: as a stylized fashion shoot and as an exploration of her own references—the femmes fatales of Taiwanese cinema, her relationship with her deaf father, or her mother's loneliness, for example.

In these shoots, Hua often constructs sets made of paper, a medium to which she was originally drawn for its accessibility; now she uses its inherent fragility to explore the constructed nature of memory. Truth, Hua knows, is only ever approximated: we create narratives in its stead. "Designing an object or a landscape as an extension of reality always comes with a story," she says. Her use of construction as metaphor rhymes with her interest in Vietnamese modernist architecture, particularly as described in the architect Phu Vinh Pham's 2021 book *Poetic Significance*, which argues that the style makes use of available modes and materials, blending rationalist function with spirituality and imagination.

Hua sees photography as a means to represent emotional truth without relying on the belief in the camera as sole witness. For her series *Tropism, Consequences of a Displaced Memory* (2016–21), Hua began by gathering archival photographs from her family's time in Vietnam and their early years in France. Using a simple algorithmic tool that fills a shape with the information around it, she then digitally manipulated these images, working without a plan, allowing the process and the feelings it evoked to guide her. "It was a sensation you can hardly materialize—so I had to find it by working on the pictures," Hua says.

Reworking the surface of the images, which Hua likens to the act of painting, mirrored her experience of filling the lacunae in her understanding of her family and Vietnamese identity. "Nothing is random," she says. "Each image is a statement that took me a while to reflect on. When the image is done, it's a way of saying that my reflection is done."

Larissa Pham is the author of *Fantasian* (2016), a novella, and *Pop Song* (2021), a collection of essays on art and intimacy.

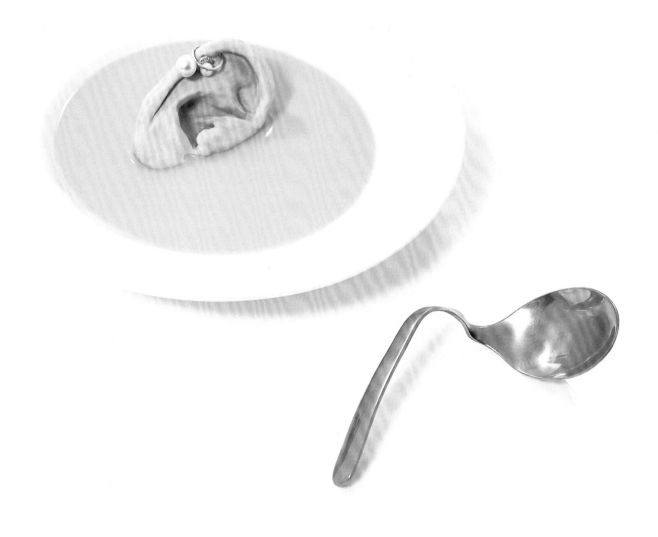

Braindead, 2016

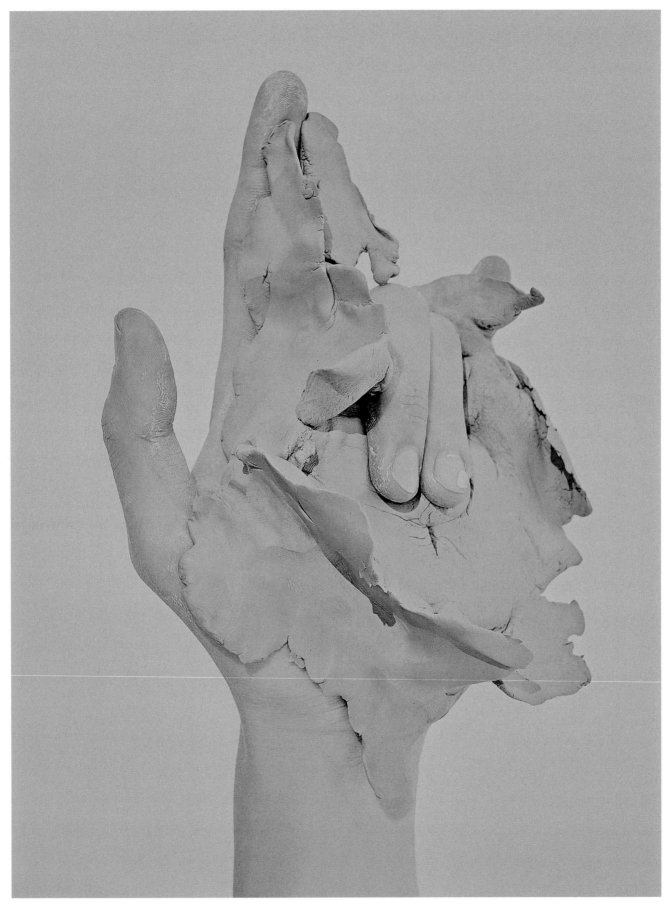

ILU, 2017

The Distorted Bench, 2019

We walked in the forest at night, 2018

Top:
Gardienne du Temple, 2020;
bottom: *The Wedding – Archive
from 1985*, 2016–21

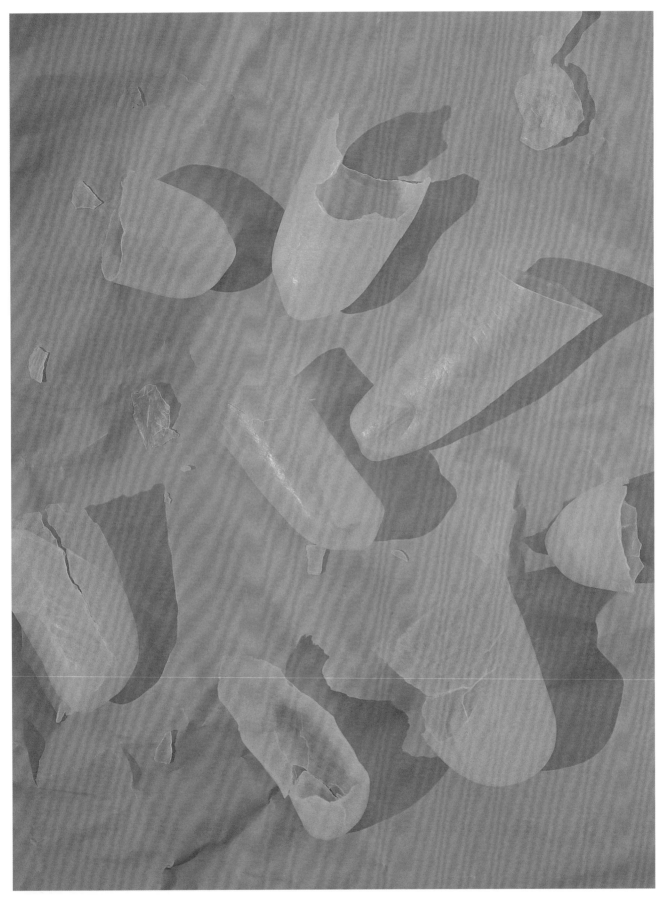

Previous spread:
Singer: "How much love can be repeated?," 2022;
this page: *Sharp Tongue, Round Fingers,* 2017

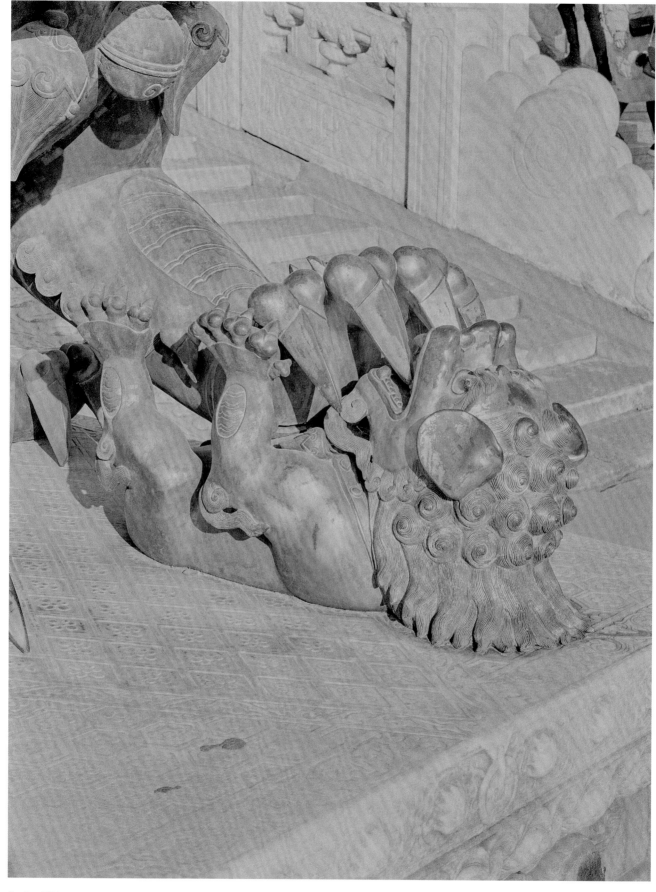

Feeding, 2018
Courtesy the artist

Untitled (Beauty Papers), 2021

Vince Aletti

For all their polish, there's something about Paul Kooiker's pictures that feels outsider, something obsessive and off. Even when he's photographing ordinary subjects—an egg, a wig, a shoe, an eyeball—in a relatively straightforward style, the results look alien. Maybe that's why the Dutch photographer, who has published nineteen books since 1999, remains a cult figure.

His latest book, *Fashion* (2023), is the source for much of the work in the portfolio that follows, and an ideal starting point for anyone curious about his oeuvre as a whole, which is so various it's difficult to pin down. Based in Amsterdam, Kooiker has a neo-Dadaist approach to subject matter, notably a deadpan take on the still life, which makes him especially appealing to brands, such as Acne, Hermès, and Rick Owens, that hope to appeal to the adventurous consumer. If he's known for anything it's his genre-smashing work with the female nude. His women tend to be large and bulky, as monumental as Botero sculptures but often collapsed, like Bill Brandt's figures in bleak interiors. These pillowy bodies don't frequently turn up in Kooiker's fashion photographs, but their occasional presence is only one way he challenges the genre's conventions.

He often treats his models like mannequins, denying them presence or personality by obscuring their heads or masking their faces. Typically, he combines live flesh and factory-made limbs in figures that recall Salvador Dalí sculptures and Horst P. Horst's surreal inventions for *Vogue*. The results—such as the female figure bent over and covered by cardboard tubes and a broad-brimmed black wig—merge the clownish and the grotesque. When we do see a head, it's often lighted like an object (see his recent alarmingly unflattering portraits of the fashion designer Jenna Lyons for *New York* magazine) or disembodied and put on a table like an offering to the gods.

It will come as no surprise that, outside of how mercilessly he can tweak it, Kooiker has no particular interest in fashion photography. Instead, he tells me, his influences come mainly from film (Rainer Werner Fassbinder, Robert Bresson, Lars von Trier) and "contemporary art, in general, especially outsider art." Plus, not so incidentally, medical, police, and crime-scene photographs. He backtracks a bit to acknowledge a real affinity with his contemporaries Juergen Teller,

The Theater of Paul Kooiker

This page:
Untitled (Bakovic Studio),
2022

Opposite:
Untitled (Studio), 2018

lous production compressed to a single scene. Others tease the idea of the "important accessory": showing an expensive leather glove on a hand grasping a slab of soft dough, strewing a fortune in jewels over what looks like a damp bath towel, or sticking five sky-high heels on an array of mannequin legs fanned out from a plaster base (Pierre Molinier's devil doll, an alter ego of the French artist, would scream with envy). The agility and wit of Kooiker's improvisations are helped, surely, by the fact that he photographs not with a camera but with a cell phone.

"All my work since 2010 has been made with iPhones," he said. "Also, all my fashion work. I started out with the iPhone 3 and from then almost every year the latest version." He's using the model 15 now and is clearly hooked. "It's not a big issue for me," Kooiker added. "I just love the flexibility and limitations of this camera phone, and, in the end, people don't see it. Most people think my work is made with analog cameras."

Kooiker is happy to remain at the outer edge of the fashion-image-making establishment, such as it is. If that means his pictures appear mostly in European, avant-garde, alternative style and culture magazines—*Acne Paper*, *Luncheon*, *Numéro*, *Dust*, *Dazed*, and *AnOther*—that also means there's a lot less compromise and editorial interference involved. Asked about photographers he related to, he named two outsider, and for some photo-world insiders, cult, figures: Hans Bellmer, the great German French Surrealist, and Gerard Fieret, the Dutch artist best known for rubber-stamping his name and address all over his slapdash erotic images. "It was a shock when I saw their work for the first time," Kooiker recalled. "I felt that I was not alone in the art world."

Roe Ethridge, and Viviane Sassen because, like him, they "stand with one leg in the art world and with the other in the fashion world." Kooiker adds, "The pleasure of making fashion pictures is, for me, the dynamic of it. You have to do it most of the time in one day, and it's never all perfect, so you have to improvise. So even when things go wrong, you have to solve it very quickly. I really like these moments of making decisions very fast without too much doubt. I also love to work on the set design, to create my own world in a small studio with cardboard, smoke, and dust."

That sense of improvisation animates all of Kooiker's output, but it's especially evident in his fashion pictures, some of which suggest a Theatre of the Ridicu-

Vince Aletti is a photography critic, writer, and curator living in New York.

Untitled (AnOther), 2021

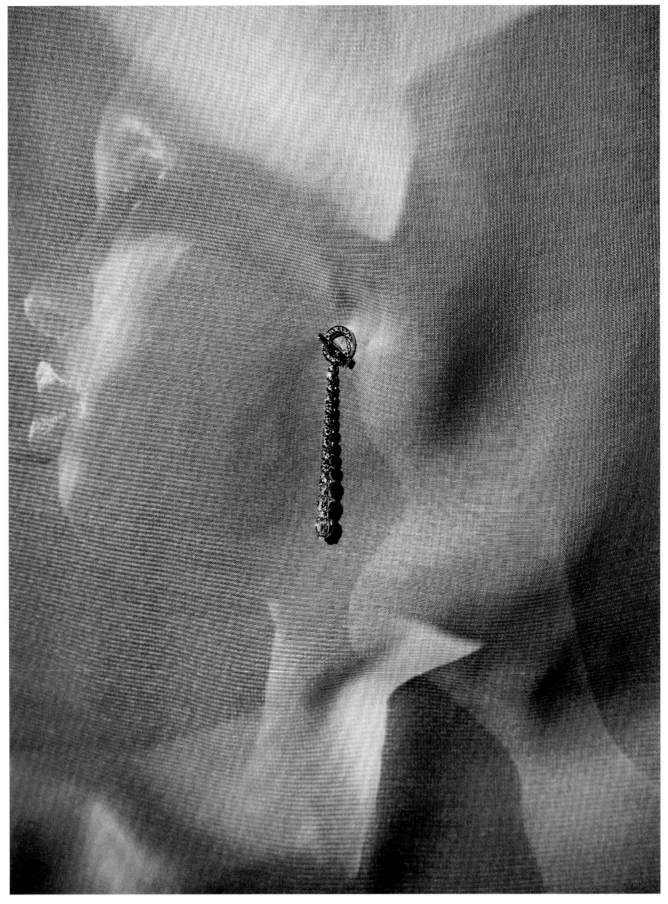

Untitled (Hermès), 2023

Untitled (Holiday), 2021

Untitled (Rianne van Rompaey), 2023

Untitled (Duran Lantink), 2020
Courtesy the artist

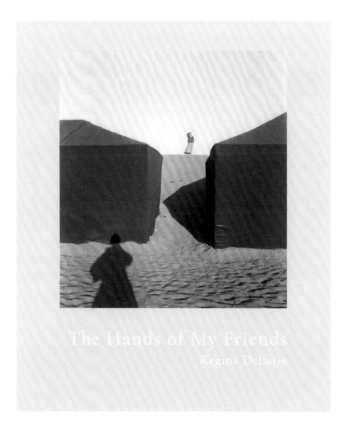

The Hands of My Friends
Regina DeLuise

mica.edu/aperture

M|I|C|A
PHOTOGRAPHY

Forthcoming from Saint Lucy Books:
embracing portraiture, landscape, and still life,
The Hands of My Friends gathers four decades
of elegant, intimate, and powerful imagery
from Regina DeLuise, Faculty Emerita,
MICA Photography. Available May 2024

saintlucybooks.com

Photography

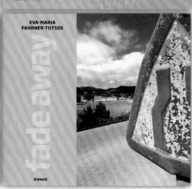

From Scheidegger & Spiess
Ernst Scheidegger
Photographer
Edited by Ernst Scheidegger Archive Foundation
Cloth $65.00

Alpine Passes of Switzerland
Journey to Modernity
Edited and with Photographs by
Richard von Tscharner
Cloth $85.00

From Hirmer Publishers
Ylla
The Birth of Modern Animal Photography
Pryor Dodge
Cloth $55.00

Eva-Maria Fahrner-Tutsek
Fade Away
Photographs by Eva-Maria Fahrner-Tutsek
Cloth $35.00

Distributed by the University of Chicago Press www.press.uchicago.edu

artbook &
distributed art publishers

DENNIS HOPPER IN DREAMS

LaToya Ruby Frazier
Monuments of Solidarity

WOMAN OF STEEL
UNITED STEELWORKERS OF AMERICA

MoMA

AMERICAN GOTHIC GORDON PARKS AND ELLA WATSON

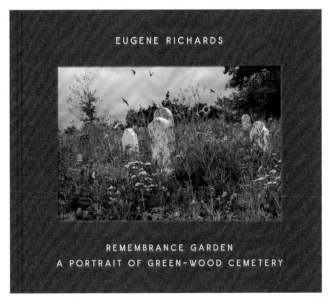

EUGENE RICHARDS

REMEMBRANCE GARDEN
A PORTRAIT OF GREEN-WOOD CEMETERY

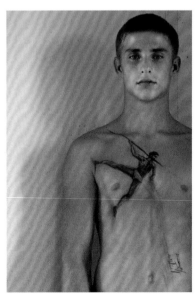

LaToya Ruby Frazier: Monuments of Solidarity, Frazier's personalized arrangements of her compelling photographs recognize the myriad social and political struggles of Black working-class communities. **THE MUSEUM OF MODERN ART, NEW YORK**

Eugene Richards: Remembrance Garden A Portrait of Green-Wood Cemetery, An exquisitely somber portrait of Brooklyn's Green-Wood cemetery across the seasons. **D.A.P.**

American Gothic: Gordon Parks and Ella Watson, An expansive look at one of the greatest American photo series. **STEIDL / THE GORDON PARKS FOUNDATION / MINNEAPOLIS INSTITUTE OF ART**

Luke Smalley: Exercise at Home, Idiosyncratic looks at the stereotype of the red-blooded American man. **TWIN PALMS PUBLISHERS**

The art world's source for books on art & culture | artbook.com

The PhotoBook Review

Poetic Research

Polymode is known for a wide variety of design projects, including books, exhibitions, and motion graphics. Dori Tunstall recently spoke with Silas Munro and Brian Johnson about founding one of the few Black- and Indigenous-led design firms.

Polymode started as a concept before becoming a business in 2014. Its co-founders, Silas Munro and Brian Johnson—who first met at RISD and have collaborated over the years from North Carolina and California—dismantle the idea of designers who leave their identities behind. By using what they call "poetic research," the partners insert their lived experiences and artistic perspectives into their work. To further this embracing mindset, the two have also founded a series of design-history courses with a BIPOC focus.

Dori Tunstall: **Can you tell us the origin story of Polymode and how it is closely intertwined with your friendship?**

Silas Munro: "Polymode" was the title of my master's thesis at CalArts, which I completed in 2008. That's where the name of the studio comes from. That thesis was about exploring the connections between a designer's identity and their visual and strategic practice. I made a series of four fictional personas as a way to break out of this know-it-all graphic-designer vibe that I came into grad school with. There was a biracial graphic designer, a bodybuilding graphic designer, a queer graphic designer, and also a philosophical graphic designer. Polymode is all about this idea of multifacetedness, shape-shifting, and different styles.

DT: **Brian, what is your version of the origin story?**

Brian Johnson: It is exactly that, and it's also how Silas and I became friends as undergrads at RISD, and how that friendship deepened when we lived together in Raleigh from 2008 to 2009. At RISD, I had seen Silas, and Silas had seen me, right? And how Silas tells it is that you could see me wearing my old Boy Scout uniform, Pride flag stitched over the American flag, dyed hair, and a little metal lunch box: the epitome of *XY* magazine, fag boy across campus at an art school in 2001. To have someone like Silas see me as vulnerable, and to be soft with me, and to realize that my bark just keeps people away because I am that little tender boy inside. Our tender boys could sit and play with Barbies and not be bothered by the cacophony of the world around us. Where it really was a brotherhood or a sisterhood. There was that level of friendship, and I feel like that's the beginning of Polymode.

SM: The "official" part was in 2014 when Lorraine Wild, who was a former teacher of mine, recommended that I work on a book-design project for the Museum of Modern Art, for the Jacob Lawrence *Migration Series*. The first person I thought to call was Brian. I was like, Oh, I want to do this project, but I can't do it by myself.

Top to bottom:
Materials from the courses
Black Design in America, 2021;
Incomplete Latinx Stories, 2021;
and Design Histories in Southwest
Asia & North Africa, 2023

DT: **You are one of the few Black- and Indigenous-led design firms in North America. What perspective does that bring to your work, both individually and as a company?**

SM: It can feel intense because we bring a lived experience that allows for unique perspectives and a way of looking at design that is not common in leadership positions in design studios. I think that's starting to shift in practice. And, at the same time, it also brings an expectation, or pressure, that you need to speak for other people who are not in the room.

When people see me, they see a Black man in America, and they don't necessarily see that my mom is a Ugandan woman who has Indigenous lineage to the Banyole people of Eastern Uganda. And so there's that, but also, my dad is white. Another thing that Brian and I have in common is an understanding of the complicated experience of what it means to have an Indigenous or marginalized experience but also a colonized lineage at the same time.

BJ: And then there's the harsher reality of everyone seeing me as white before they see me as Indigenous. And it's a really

This page:
Cover of *Jacob Lawrence:
The Migration Series* (New
York: Museum of Modern
Art, 2017); opposite:
Spread from Silas Munro,
"poly-mode: A Mutable
System of Graphic Design
Strategies" (master's
thesis, CalArts, 2008)

We bring a way of looking at design that is not common in leadership positions.

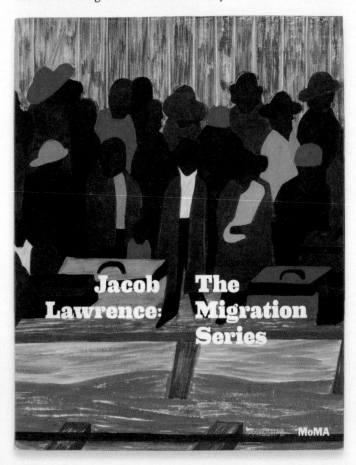

hard thing when you already have a couple of generations of family that had to pass as white because of miscegenation laws. If you wanted to even get married or own property and not be a sharecropper, you had to pass as white. And then you add the queerness in, that "divine kiss of queerness," as we call it. You're already othered. There is room, and there is space enough, but you also have to make it. You have to share that, and you have to teach other people. That is one of the unique perspectives we are trying to bring to this business writ large that doesn't want to share that way. It can be a challenge.

DT: **In the DNA of Polymode, again, you talk about connecting your lived experience and who you are to the work you do. That's the underlying essence. Compared to other companies, how did the events in response to the murder of George Floyd in 2020 change you? Is there a pre-2020 and post-2020 Polymode?**

SM: Part of the pre-2020 version of Polymode had to do with bandwidth, scope, and scale. As I mentioned already, our first project was about Jacob Lawrence, a Black artist who had ties to the Harlem Renaissance and the Great Migration. And, as the book was going into design and production, there was also the emergence of Black Lives Matter, Ferguson, and pre–George Floyd. These shifts in culture were happening.

Before George Floyd, we, like other colleagues, were already doing research into histories of Black and Indigenous folks, including W. E. B. Du Bois. As soon as George Floyd happened, suddenly there was that urgency to expand opportunity access—a need for designers and creative people who could speak in these new ways. We went from having two to having nine projects to having thirty projects.

BJ: It was like being strapped to a Saturn V rocket. I mean, the trajectory was insane. But because we have this ability to shape-shift and to be proactive, we can also meld around those things and make it work, and juggle and be light on our feet, quicken how we think, and not waste time and energy.

DT: **Let's talk about poetic research. What is it, and how did it start?**

BJ: Ooh, what is it? Poetic research is everything and the kitchen sink, because how do you define it? The poetic research is everything that the client can give you about a subject. What are the images? What are the essays? But then it's, What does it make me think of? So, it makes me think of this object, this piece of music, this museum show, this color, this food that I'm eating. But it also makes me think about the book of poetry on my bedside table.

SM: I think how it's distinct from other forms of research is the part of bringing in, again, the experience of the designer. What are we also thinking about or reading? Or, how does the particular project brief inspire us? It's like a call-and-response between our own personal references and the client's point of view.

DT: **Can you give me three examples of poetic research and, particularly, how it changed the trajectory of a project in three flavors? One flavor is a basic request. How did you address that basic request through poetic research? And**

how did that shift the outcome? The second flavor is a project that was hopelessly complex or confusing. And last, the third flavor is something that was community driven.

BJ: I got a basic one. We were asked to help redesign the website for the Frye Art Museum, in Seattle, but it turned into a rebranding, and we didn't mean for it to. We were just looking at contemporary websites for an art museum at that scale. Silas and I went to the museum, we explored and took pictures of textures. We looked at this kind of iridescent metal. We looked at the typography in different stages of the building and showed the client how it shifted, and then found a brother-sister typeface that also has a little bit of nuance to it. They realized by the colors, typography, and textures we presented that, Oh, no, this is not about a website. This is about a brand refresh.

SM: I can talk about the more complex example, and it's connected to an upcoming book with Aperture that is an index of Paul Mpagi Sepuya's work. We realized

that to actually create the book, Paul and I needed to do these sessions together where we were working on the book in real time. And so that actually did change the scope of the project and extended the timeline, but it created this design that could not have happened in any other way.

DT: **And the community driven . . . ?**

SM and BJ: [*simultaneously*] BIPOC Design History!

SM: How do you actually create a new way of thinking about a design-history curriculum? But also, how do you rethink what a design school is? Or about the way that histories are taught and learned? I started posting on social media asking if people would want to attend a course centering on BIPOC voices. The course became a one-room schoolhouse where we were all learning from one another, and the community was actually shaping the research, not just the structure of it but, literally, the knowledge was this community-crafted structure. And then

Installation view of
*Deconstructing Power:
W. E. B. Du Bois at the
1900 World's Fair*, Cooper
Hewitt, Smithsonian
Design Museum, New York,
2022–23, with design by
Polymode. Photograph
by David Bartolomi
Courtesy Polymode

we also shared the profits with the co-instructors.

BJ: We're trying to make sure that it's the most affordable for those who are the most harmed. So anyone of color doesn't have to pay full price. It's not business as usual, it's business as different.

DT: **What's next for Polymode?**

SM: It's about scale and impact and bringing Polymode to a new level. As we keep collaborating, we find that Polymode has now become something that's bigger than Brian or me. And even though we are technically the officers of the structure, the studio is starting to shift so that it is also a school, meaning we are teaching everyone at Polymode how to do our jobs in a way.

BJ: Our value has gone up, and many institutions are like, How dare you ask for more money? Even when you start to get into these big multimillion-dollar companies, they still don't want to pay more. We're trying to figure out how we can shift and still be relevant. Also, how can we take care of our whole team and not

burn everybody out because we have to take on more projects to have more capital to expand and grow this idea of Polymode? It's a perpetual dialogue.

Elizabeth "Dori" Tunstall is a writer, educator, and design anthropologist.

Elements of Style

A new book shows why Alexey Brodovitch's innovative art direction has never gone out of fashion.

Christina Cacouris

Paging through vintage magazines feels like falling into a time warp. The cost of fashion and beauty products alone is boggling ($6.95 for suede gloves! $15 for a wool dress!). They serve as unique capsules from a bygone era of style and fantasy, a time when the people at the helm could make or break artistic careers. One such kingmaker was Alexey Brodovitch, whose art direction for *Harper's Bazaar*, across decades, from the mid-1930s through the 1950s, set a new standard for graphic design and photography in magazines.

The recent book *Alexey Brodovitch: Astonish Me* (**Yale University Press, 2024; 174 pages, $50**), which accompanied an exhibition last spring at the Barnes Foundation in Philadelphia, demonstrates the breadth of not only

Brodovitch's career but of his artistic prowess, from paintings and lithographs to art direction and photography.

But how does one go about designing a book on one of the twentieth century's most prolific and significant designers?

There are nods to Brodovitch's style throughout *Astonish Me*, beginning with the title—his favorite exhortation. The foreword's text is slanted to mirror an October 1934 *Harper's Bazaar* spread that he designed. And the headings' typeface is an homage to the type stretching across the cover of Brodovitch's own 1945 photobook, *Ballet*. "Brodovitch was very laconic, apart from a couple of articles he wrote, so there was a bit of detective work in thinking about how to represent someone via unconventional means or via the stories and materials from other people who knew him," says Katy Wan, who curated the exhibition and edited the catalog. *Astonish Me* is divided into four parts: Brodovitch's early life and artwork, the *Harper's Bazaar* years, his independent art direction, and, finally, *Ballet*, photographs from which grace the book's slipcase and back cover.

This page:
Spread from the *Ninth Ballet Theatre Annual* (Charles Payne, 1949), with photographs by Richard Avedon; opposite: Alexey Brodovitch reviewing page layouts for *Observations*, 1959. Photograph by Richard Avedon
© Richard Avedon Foundation

Look closely and you'll see that Brodovitch's influence is omnipresent in today's media.

Ballet, Brodovitch's only photobook, remains one of the most revolutionary of the form, and the rare copies that resurface sell for thousands of dollars today. From the whirling gyre of *The Sylphs (Les Sylphides)* to the flight of *Les Noces (The Wedding)*, Brodovitch's photographs are far from sublunary. The blurred images— an act of defiance against the progressive sharpening of photography—transform the dancers into ethereal beings. But the photographs are only half the innovation, as David Campany points out in an essay for *Astonish Me*. Brodovitch printed them in full bleed across spread after spread without margins as buffers, breaking only to introduce the next sequence in the dance, with each title presented in its own dedicated typeface. (*Les Noces* is bold, whereas the airy *Cotillion* is all white, with light-black shadows shaping each letter.)

And yet, none of *Ballet*'s influence is directly felt in the projects Brodovitch oversaw at *Harper's Bazaar* or in the books he art directed. "There isn't a stylistic or aesthetic unity between the work of his students and his associates," Wan

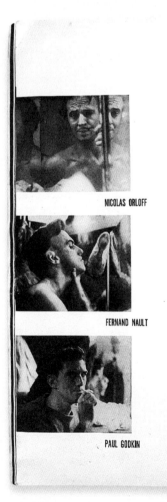

NICOLAS ORLOFF

FERNAND NAULT

PAUL GODKIN

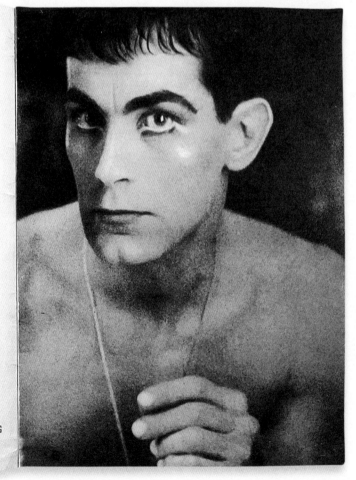

HUGH LAING

Cover of André Kertész,
Day of Paris (J. J. Augustine,
1945), with jacket design
by Alexey Brodovitch
Courtesy the Barnes
Foundation, Philadelphia

says. Brodovitch's eclectic and brightly visual design for *Portfolio: A Magazine for the Graphic Arts*, particularly in a 1951 spread on Jackson Pollock, with photographs by Hans Namuth, feels incongruous with the quiet elegance of his approach to Lillian Bassman's images at *Harper's Bazaar*. He wasn't imposing his own vision: he was helping draw out the genius he saw within his collaborators.

Although he's not a household name—hopefully *Astonish Me* will rectify that—Brodovitch has been the subject of previous shows and publications, most notably the 1972 exhibition and book *Alexey Brodovitch and His Influence*, the latter of which opened with a series of quotes from his former students. Richard Avedon: "I learned from his impatience, his arrogance, his dissatisfaction." Irving Penn: "Within these austere and forbidding circumstances, when the student did somehow manage to push forward into new ground, Brodovitch glumly, even grudgingly left no doubt that something remarkable had been done. And it seemed that the very sparseness of his recognition lent it an intensity of meaning and importance hard to explain to someone who did not actually experience it."

Astonish Me includes similar testimony, and Wan was intent on displaying Brodovitch as the difficult character he is reputed to have been. "I would like to pose the question, without fully resolving it, of whether that, in fact, challenges creatives to strive to be the absolute best they can be," she explains.

Look closely and you'll see that Brodovitch's influence is omnipresent in today's media: His inclusion of artists' work in fashion magazines has become de rigueur. And in an age when seemingly every brand has adopted a new sans serif logo, it is significant that *Harper's Bazaar* still uses the same Didot typeface that Brodovitch brought to its masthead. But one wonders where the Brodovitch of today is, or if he even exists; as fashion magazines are thinner, budgets grow tighter, and production moves faster, the halcyon days of mentors such as Brodovitch (or his Condé Nast counterpart, Alexander Liberman) educing groundbreaking photography from the next generation seem far behind us. Avedon tried to keep the flame alive in 1967, teaching his Master Class alongside the art director Marvin Israel, but it was short-lived. Brodovitch's wonderfully weird, playful, and striking vision inspires a longing for the past. The luster of glossy magazines has dimmed, but it hasn't gone out entirely; we can be astonished once again.

Christina Cacouris is a writer based in Paris.

The Designer's Bookshelf

There are proper photobooks, showcasing the work of a single photographer's accomplishments, and then there are books that use photography in the service of something else, as a manual, guide, illustration, or history lesson. For this issue, we invited a group of graphic designers to select some of their favorite books that use photographs to delve into a range of ideas related to design.

Sonya Dyakova

The Art of Papercraft (**B. T. Batsford, 1971**) by Hiroshi Ogawa is a comprehensive guide to the Japanese art of paper sculpture. It contains more than 110 photographs, with great attention to detail. The images are dramatic and atmospheric, as if the sculptures are suspended in space and time. The black background and soft shadows enhance the beauty of the shapes. Ogawa provides not only general instructions and suggestions but also explanatory illustrations and notes to accompany the photographs, making this book a practical resource for anyone interested in paper sculpture. It's special to see the way humble materials and simple techniques can come together to create something so powerful.
—**Sonya Dyakova is the founder of Atelier Dyakova, a design studio in London.**

Duncan Whyte

The Most Beautiful Swiss Books (**Federal Office of Culture, Bern**) is an annual publication documenting a yearly competition. The volumes are always fascinating, with a Swiss budget for epic reproduction. The two volumes with the best photographs are from 2016 and 2022: 2016 is devoted to "examination," with spreads comparing all the nominated books through thirty or so different criteria, including spine, strength, and pagination; 2022 features a moody fashion shoot for each book.
—**Duncan Whyte is an independent art book designer living and working in France.**

1941, Sherman M. Fairchild House, 17 East 65th Street. This house represented a new use of the city lot: the front entertaining rooms are separated from the rear bedrooms by a garden court not seen from the street. The concept was used again in 1951 when Philip Johnson built a similar house for John D. Rockefeller, Jr., at 242 East 52nd Street. The wartime fashion silhouette, limited by fabric shortages, concentrated on padded square shoulders, the page-boy hairstyle, and platform shoes.

Opposite, 1943, Times Square. A wartime fantasy among the flashing billboards was the strapless sarong inspired by the native costumes of Java and Ceylon that GIs had sent back home to waiting girlfriends. The fashion world was soon manufacturing homegrown sarongs in exotic flower-pattern fabrics. The pompadour hairstyle was the rage as were high platform-sole shoes.

Jordan Marzuki

Aliens and Herons **(Arbor Vitae, 2016)** by Pavel Karous is a guidebook documenting postcommunist public art throughout the Czech Republic. The book employs its own taxonomy—class, order, family, genus, and species—to identify each artwork, along with beautifully structured typography and colorful pages. Cheeky illustrations contribute to an unconventional and hilarious narrative, in stark contrast to the serious, often dark history of the region.
—**Jordan Marzuki is a designer based in Jakarta, Indonesia, and the founder of Jordan, jordan Édition.**

Pavel Karous ed.

Vetřelci a volavky

Atlas výtvarného umění ve veřejném prostoru v Československu v období normalizace (1968–1989)

Aliens and Herons

A Guide to Fine Art in the Public Space in the Era of Normalisation (1968–1989)

Other Means

Bill Cunningham's *Facades* **(Penguin, 1978)** features 128 photographs of his neighbor Editta Sherman posing in front of buildings in New York City, wearing period-correct outfits Bill collected over ten years. In most cases the buildings and clothing are in harmony, with the exception of the Twin Towers—Bill contrasts the clean, austere modernism of the towers with the "raunchy" blue jeans culture of the time. Our favorite photographs show Editta next to a graffiti-covered subway, illustrating the book's core concept of the city as a collage of design spanning two hundred years. The cover, designed by Quentin Fiore, is printed in brilliant red and blue spot colors on metallic paper, evoking Midtown Manhattan's reflective facades.
—**Other Means, a design studio in New York, was founded by Ryan Waller, Gary Fogelson, and Phil Lubliner.**

WORK/PLAY

For us, *Ghetto Gastro Presents Black Power Kitchen* **(Artisan, 2022)** is more than just a cookbook. We love how the chefs incorporate experimental recipes along with new takes on traditional recipes and the histories behind these meals. The pages are culturally immersed in who we are as Black people and are showcased through a Black cultural lens. From the Bronx to destinations all across the globe, Ghetto Gastro is bringing "food for freedom, fuel for thought."
—**WORK/PLAY is an interdisciplinary design studio cofounded by Danielle and Kevin McCoy and based in St. Louis, Missouri.**

Vera Lucía Jiménez

I first learned about ***Puruchuco*** (**Editorial Organización de Promociones Culturales, Lima, ca. 1981**) from a beautiful piece written by the Peruvian poet Jorge Eduardo Eielson. Illustrated with photographs by José Casals, *Puruchuco* shows, with words and images, the attempt to rethink an architectural complex on the coast of Peru that belonged to the Inca Empire from the thirteenth century and served as an administrative center and house of the curaca, an elite official. Casals's images detail the precision and sensitivity of pre-Hispanic architecture: places connected to the corporality of the inhabitant and the uses they gave to the spaces.

—Vera Lucía Jiménez is a publication designer who works between Lima, Peru, and Porto, Portugal.

Maricris Herrera

Roberto Luna's photographs of the architect Francisco Artigas's houses published in ***Francisco Artigas*** (**Tlaloc, 1972**) are distinguished by their challenging of traditional visual conventions and their exploration of new forms of architectural expression. With remarkable boldness, Luna constructs insightful narratives for utopian scenarios, revealing his unique ability to fuse modern aesthetics with functionality [see page 145]. Beyond his architecture, Artigas's distinctive style of self-presentation stands out for its innovation and, above all, its provocative character.

—Maricris Herrera established the Mexico City–based design practice Estudio Herrera in 2016.

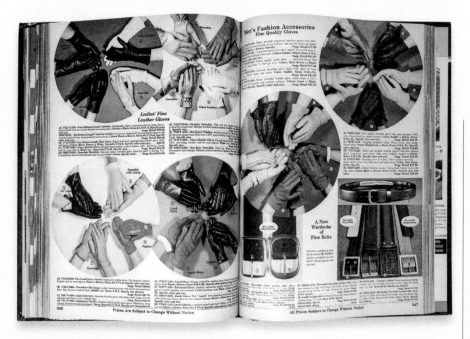

Adam Turnbull

I was drawn to this publication—the ***Blue Book of Quality Merchandise 1980*** (**Bennett Brothers, 1980**)—because of the product imagery. I love how the photographs are art directed and the products styled: the hands wearing the gloves, the staged still lifes, the radios with the dark gradient background. The repetition of the products laid out on the page creates a beautiful rhythm. It's an amazing relic of a piece of marketing material that was both functional and pleasing.

—Adam Turnbull is the cofounder, with Elizabeth Karp-Evans, of Pacific, a creative studio in New York.

Gabrielle Guy

I happened to be living in Johannesburg at the time that ***UP UP: Stories of Johannesburg's Highrises*** (**Fourthwall, 2016**) came out. I found the city fascinating—so different from Cape Town, where I'm from. The city center is big and run-down, and so much more ambitious architecturally. I remember going to the book launch, held in a cool space in Braamfontein on the outskirts of the Central Business District. I love how the book manages to incorporate old and new photographs, architectural illustrations, and archival documents. It's difficult to deal with such a range of visual material in layout, yet *UP UP*, with its solid grid, strong typeface, and rigid approach to sections and binding manages to create a strong aesthetic.

—Gabrielle Guy is an art book designer and artist based in Cape Town, South Africa.

Akiko Wakabayashi

Kurashi no souzou, **no. 7 (Sogei Shuppan, 1978)** is the design magazine's special issue on Japanese craft. For me, the most attractive element is the cover image. The still life on the front is mirrored and then layered twice on the back. One section is treated with a distortion effect. Was this a mistake, a conscious experiment with technique, or is there a hidden conceptual message? The result is puzzling, but this mysterious outcome raises a lot of questions, which I love.
—**Akiko Wakabayashi is an independent designer based in the Netherlands.**

Alex Lin

I found *The Pill Book* **(Bantam, 2012),** which covers more than 1,800 of the most regularly prescribed drugs in the United States, to be an effective use of photography as a reference for people. It's a really beautiful and practical book, which runs more than 1,200 pages. I think it's also great that the pills are printed to scale.
—**Alex Lin established Studio Lin, a Brooklyn-based graphic design practice, in 2012.**

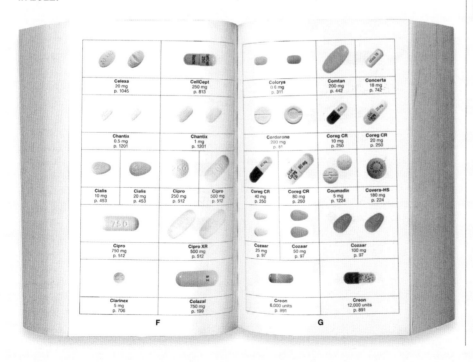

Scott Williams

The Powers of Ten **(W. H. Freeman & Co., 1998)** is a flipbook depicting stills from a film of the same name, created by the office of Charles and Ray Eames in 1977. The book is a conceptual and pictorial journey that starts at the edge of the universe and hurtles down to Earth, at tenfold steps, with a photograph depicting each interval along the way. The camera descends rapidly to Earth until the lens eventually enters the hand of a man lounging at a picnic at a park on Lake Shore Drive, Chicago, down into his cells, his DNA, and finally to a single proton. It's a small book with a big idea.
—**Scott Williams is cofounder, with Henrik Kubel, of A2/SW/HK, a design studio in London.**

Endnote
Olivia Laing

Olivia Laing has established herself as one of our most exacting cultural critics. Her new book, *The Garden Against Time: In Search of a Common Paradise*, uses the restoration of her own eighteenth-century walled garden as a starting point to consider how we might imagine paradise.

Edwin Smith, *Villa Garzoni, Collodi: console on the third terrace with female figure of a goat-legged satyr*, 1962
Courtesy the artist/RIBA Collections

How did your new book on gardens and paradise begin?
I've been working on it since 2020, but the initial stages were restoring the physical garden itself and keeping a garden diary. I originally trained as a herbalist, so I've been thinking about plants and utopia for a long time.

The book is part memoir, part cultural history. There's one section where you describe botany as an education in looking.
Yes, a very fine-grained looking, where you're looking with precision to identify and differentiate—which isn't the only kind of looking I'm interested in anymore.

How much did the change and calamity of the pandemic shift your focus?
The intense isolation of the pandemic happening at the same time as issues such as Black Lives Matter, and that entire conversation about physical space—who gets to use it, who owns it, whose labor paid for it—definitely shaped the book.

You talk about the many symbolic roles of the garden as Eden, the tension between "the world as it is and the world as we want it to be." And you include rebels in the garden, such as the Diggers.
The Diggers were enormously influential to the road protests and environmental-activism movement that I was involved in during the 1990s. These seventeenth-century radicals practiced a kind of land-based communism way before communism was invented.

You also write about the filmmaker Derek Jarman.
In his 1991 book *Modern Nature*, Jarman articulates the idea of being excluded from paradise as a gay child at public school, and feeling this great need to reclaim and make his own alternative Eden. One of those alternative Edens was Hampstead Heath, where he goes to cruise, and the other was his improbable garden at Prospect Cottage.

What was in your research dossier?
Random images collected as I went along. Seventeenth-century woodcuts of Adam and Eve. Some amazing photographs from the Blitz in World War II London, with girls sunbathing amid ruins and flowers. Mughal miniatures. A Thomas Gainsborough. A beautiful photograph of Cedric Morris gardening, surrounded by irises. I didn't really know how they connected, but I knew they belonged together.

You're an admirer of Edwin Smith's photographs of gardens. Why?
Well, I feel like he is a genius at conveying the atmosphere of a place, and how you would feel inside it. They've got such a distorted, surreal strangeness about them.

You talk about the tension between the artifice of the garden and the wildness of the garden, which are all elements of design.
The most interesting thing about design for me is the parallel between garden making and writing. My garden is divided by hedges with archways cut in them. You can never see everything all at once. I wanted to replicate that with the design of the book, so that when you enter into a new chapter, it's at once discrete and related to everything else. You've walked in there from the previous chapter. You're connected.

How is the work on your own actual garden coming along? Is the garden done now?
[*Laughs*] I mean, is it ever done?